The Big Book of Therapeutic Activity Ideas for Children and Teens

of related interest

Games and Activities for Exploring Feelings
Vanessa Rogers
ISBN 978 1 84905 222 1

How to Be Angry
An Assertive Anger Expression Group Guide for Kids and Teens
Signe Whitson
Foreword by Dr. Nicholas Long
ISBN 978 1 84905 867 4

Creating Children's Art Games for Emotional Support
Vicky Barber
ISBN 978 1 84905 163 7

Creative Coping Skills for Children
Emotional Support through Arts and Crafts Activities
Bonnie Thomas
ISBN 978 1 84310 921 1

Creative Expression Activities for Teens
Exploring Identity through Art, Craft and Journaling
Bonnie Thomas
ISBN 978 1 84905 842 1

Helping Children to Improve their Communication Skills
Therapeutic Activities for Teachers, Parents and Therapists
Deborah M. Plummer
Illustrated by Alice Harper
ISBN 978 1 84310 959 4

Helping Children to Cope with Change, Stress and Anxiety
A Photocopiable Activities Book
Deborah M. Plummer
Illustrated by Alice Harper
ISBN 978 1 84310 959 4

The Expressive Arts Activity Book
A Resource for Professionals
Suzanne Darley and Wende Heath
Illustrated by Mark Darley
Foreword by Gene D. Cohen MD PhD.
ISBN 978 1 84310 861 0

Arts Activities for Children and Young People in Need
Helping Children to Develop Mindfulness, Spiritual Awareness and Self-Esteem
Diana Coholic
ISBN 978 1 84905 001 2

The Big Book of Therapeutic Activity Ideas for Children and Teens

Inspiring Arts-Based Activities and Character Education Curricula

Lindsey Joiner

Jessica Kingsley *Publishers*
London and Philadelphia

Scripture on p.5 is taken from THE HOLY BIBLE, NEW INTERNATIONAL VERSION®, NIV® Copyright © 1973, 1978, 1984, 2011 by Biblica, Inc.™ Used by permission. All rights reserved worldwide.
Activities on p.73, pp.236–237 and pp.238–239 are adapted by permission of Joe Ray Underwood and Nancy Underwood.
Quotation by Duke Ellington on p.104 is reproduced by permission of Scarola Malone & Zubatov LLP.

First published in 2012
by Jessica Kingsley Publishers
116 Pentonville Road
London N1 9JB, UK
and
400 Market Street, Suite 400
Philadelphia, PA 19106, USA

www.jkp.com

Library of Congress Cataloging in Publication Data
A CIP catalog record for this book is available from the Library of Congress

British Library Cataloguing in Publication Data
A CIP catalogue record for this book is available from the British Library

ISBN 978 1 84905 865 0

Printed and bound in the United States

To Win and Drake

For nothing is impossible with God.

Luke 1:37

Contents

ACKNOWLEDGEMENTS 11

INTRODUCTION 13

Chapter 1 Opening Activities: Warm-Ups, Icebreakers, and Other Brief Activities   17

Picture Prompts	18	Journal Jars	29
Initially Yours	20	Journal Jams	30
It's a Dog's Life	22	Covered with Love Journals	31
What's the Story?	24	**CIRCLE TIME IDEAS**	**32**
CREATIVE FORMS OF JOURNALING	**25**	Sign In and Begin	32
Gratitude Journals	26	Stories and Snacks/Chips and Chapters/	
Art Journals	27	Books and Breakfast	33
UP Day, DOWN Day Journals	28	"Beanie Baby" Beginnings	34

Chapter 2 Cinematherapy and Bibliotherapy Activities   35

CINEMATHERAPY ACTIVITIES	**36**	*Alexander and the Terrible, Horrible, No*	
The Blind Side	36	*Good, Very Bad Day* by Judith Viorst	49
Legally Blonde	38	*The True Story of the Three Little Pigs*	
The Wizard of Oz	40	by Jon Scieszka	52
A Raisin in the Sun by Lorraine Hansberry	43	*Purplicious* by Victoria Kann and	
Mean Girls	45	Elizabeth Kann	54
BIBLIOTHERAPY ACTIVITIES	**47**	*Enemy Pie* by Derek Munson	57
If by Rudyard Kipling	47	*Rainbow Fish* by Marcus Pfister	60

Chapter 3 Therapeutic Arts Activities   64

Timeline	65	Removing the Mask	78
City of Hope	67	Positive/Negative Word Walls	80
Mosaic Mascots	69	Soul Shine Sunshine	81
Knocking Down Negativity	71	Bead Meaning Bracelets	82
Quote Quests	72	Zoo Crew/Jungle People	83
Crush the Can'ts, Raise Your Cans	73	Creative Cookbook	84
Color Coding	74	What's Bugging Me?	85
Dream/Goal Boards	75	Social Butterflies	87
Dear Younger Self	77		

JANUARY   90
Chinese Dragons (New Year's Day)   90
"I Have a Dream" Day (Dr. Martin Luther
    King, Jr.'s Birthday)   93
Recipe for Success/"When Dreams Come
    True" Day (Dr. Martin Luther King,
    Jr.'s Birthday)   95
FEBRUARY   100
Stuffed with Love (Valentine's Day)   100
Candy Cards (Valentine's Day)   102
Rhythm and Blues (Black History Month)   104
Black History Program (Black History Month)   105
MARCH   106
Pot of Gold Scavenger Hunt (St. Patrick's Day)   106
Take a (Spring) Break and Relax (Spring
    Break)   107
APRIL   109
April Showers Bring May Flowers   109
Peaceful Earth (Earth Day)   110
MAY   111
Growing a Garden of Mental Health
    (Children's Mental Health Week)   111
Step by Step (Gardening Activities)   113

JUNE   115
Bead Buddies   115
Anger-Control Totem Poles   116
JULY   127
Group Sand Castles   127
Sand Art   128
AUGUST   129
Back to School Survival Kit   129
School Pride Guide   131
SEPTEMBER   132
Tailgate Party   132
Family Tree (Grandparents' Day)   134
OCTOBER   136
Safety Spiders (Halloween)   136
Painted Pumpkins (Halloween)   138
Scaring Away Bad Behavior (Halloween)   139
NOVEMBER   140
Thankful Turkey (Thanksgiving Day)   140
Giving Back Baskets (Thanksgiving Day)   142
DECEMBER   143
Warm Hands, Warm Hearts   143
Polar Express   145

Chapter 5 Therapeutic Day Camp Activities and Day Program Ideas   147

GOAL-SETTING THERAPEUTIC CAMP SERIES   149
Recipe for success   149
Camp 1: Getting Excited about Goal Setting   150
Camp 2: Getting Our Goals on Paper   151
Camp 3: Maintaining Motivation by
    Developing Good Character   152
Camp 4: Making a Plan for Continued
    Goal Setting   153
Camp 5: Celebrating Good Behavior and
    Goal Achievement   154
Activities   155
Preliminary Goal Setting (Camp 1)   155
Spirit Banner (Camp 1)   156

Group Cheers/Chants (Camp 1)   157
Banking on Goal Setting (Camp 1)   158
Goal Progress Check (Goal Tree)
    (Camps 2, 3 and 4)   159
Positive Parachute (Camp 2)   160
Poster Goal Commitment (Camp 2)   161
The Butterfly Story (Camp 2)   162
Sticks and Stones (Camp 3)   164
Mirror, Mirror (Camp 3)   165
Excellent Egg Relay Race (Camp 3)   166
Dream Catchers (Camp 4)   167
Action Steps Windsocks (Camp 4)   168
Bead Bowl (Camp 4)   169

Good Behavior and Goal Achievement
Ceremony (Camp 5)   170

**Handouts and forms for goal setting with
children at camps**   **172**

Therapeutic Camp—Goal Criteria   172

**Ideas for adapting goal-setting camp
activities to other settings**   **178**

Sample Weekly Schedule for Goal-Setting
Curriculum and Activities   179

SELF-ESTEEM, ANGER-CONTROL, AND IMPULSE-
CONTROL THERAPEUTIC CAMP SERIES   **183**

Making me the best I can be   **183**

Camp 1: Kick Off Summer Pep Rally   184

Camp 2: Anger Control/Afternoon Reward   185

Camp 3: Self-Esteem   187

Camp 4: Impulse Control/Afternoon Reward   189

Camp 5: Reward Camp/Closing Ceremony   191

Activities   **192**

Positive Word Wall (Camp 2)   192

The Color of Anger (Camp 2)   194

Animal Anger-Control Questionnaire (Camp 2)   196

Create a Group Totem Pole (Camp 2)   198

Pull a Duck (Camp 3)   200

Carousel Ride and Face Painting (Camp 3)   202

Silent and Verbal Water Balloon Toss (Camp 3)   203

Kite Decorating and Flying (Camp 3)   205

Gardening (Camp 4)   206

"Great," "Could-Be-Better," and
"Unacceptable" Behavior Bean
Bag Toss (Camp 4)   207

Concrete Block/Stepping Stone (Camp 4)   210

**Ideas for adapting camp activities to other
settings**   **213**

POSITIVE-THINKING AND COPING-SKILLS
THERAPEUTIC CAMP SERIES   **215**

The colors of me   **215**

Camp 1: Green Camp/Positive Thinking   216

Camp 2: Red Camp/Self-Discovery   217

Camp 3: Blue Camp/Stress Relief and
Relaxation   218

Camp 4: White Camp/Peacemaking and
Conflict Resolution   219

Camp 5: Gold Camp/Reward and Closing
Ceremony   220

Activities   **221**

Positive Planter (Camp 1)   221

Positive Words Rock Garden (Camp 1)   223

Positive Words Beading (Camp 1)   224

Bead Buddies (Camp 2)   225

Stuffed with Love (Camp 2)   226

Potato Sack Race (Camp 2)   227

Taste Test (Camp 2)   228

Relaxation Music (Camp 3)   229

Sand Art (Camp 3)   230

Aromatherapy (Camp 3)   231

Group Sand Castles (Camp 3)   232

Peacing it Together (Camp 4)   234

Umbrella of Peace (Camp 4)   236

Peace Sign Design (Camp 4)   238

**Ideas for adapting camp activities to other
settings**   **243**

Ideas for therapeutic day programs   **245**

RESOURCES 248

INDEX OF PURPOSES OF ACTIVITIES. 249

Acknowledgements

It takes a village to raise a child.

African Proverb

Raising children and being a parent has been on my mind a lot lately. I am eight months pregnant with my first child as I write these words. The upcoming birth of my own child has caused me to consider how blessed I am to have a loving family and extended supportive system in my life as my husband and I begin this new phase of our lives.

While we both want to be the best parents we can be, it is a comforting feeling to know that there are grandparents, great-grandparents, aunts, uncles, cousins, pastors, and friends there when extra support is needed. As I have been reflecting on raising children, I began to think of the many ways that writing a book is like raising a child. Although my name is on the front cover, I am indebted to so many people who guided, mentored, and supported me along the way. This book would not be here today without each of you. I am so grateful to each of you.

- Dr. Lee Lee Marlow. Thank you for taking a chance on me as Day Treatment Supervisor. I know I wasn't the most likely candidate for the job, but I am forever grateful for the opportunity, and for you as one of my best friends.

- Linda Hopkins. Thank you for showing me what it means to be creative and to be a mentor. I learned more about counseling, creativity, and life from watching you than you will ever know. I am sure you will recognize some of the activities in this book.

- The MAP Camp Committee (Linda, Keisha, Latina, Lashonda, John, and Latasha) and all the staff at Weems Community Mental Health Center, Division of Children and Youth. I learned so much from each of you. Thank you for supporting me and giving me a chance.

- The children and youth at Weems Community Mental Health Center. It is my privilege to know each of you. Thank you for all you taught me. I am a better person for knowing each of you.

- The staff at the Meridian Public School District, Office of Exceptional Child Education. I am blessed to work daily with a group of knowledgeable and caring people. You each make me want to be a better person daily.

- Dr. Julia Porter. Thank you for being a mentor in the true sense of the word. You encouraged me several years ago to put all of the creative activities I used into a book. Your words of encouragement went a long way.

- Rosanne Nunnery. Thank you for showing me how to be a good day treatment supervisor. I am thankful to have you as a friend.

- Rosie Davis. Thank you to the most talented (and certainly the nicest) artist I know. The art you provided for this book exceeded my expectations. You have made many things I envisioned a reality and I am very grateful.

- Stephen Jones and Caroline Walton. Thank you for all your guidance, encouragement, and feedback. I am most appreciative for the opportunity to work with both of you.

- My wonderful family and friends. Thank you for all your support and love. I am especially grateful to my grandparents, Ruth and Charles Naylor. They sacrificed to give me many opportunities I would not otherwise have had. Words cannot express how appreciative I am for all you have done for me.

- My husband, Win. I think you know me better than I know myself. Thank you for believing in me when I did not believe in myself and for always having the right word at the right time. I am truly blessed.

Introduction

All children are artists. The problem is how to remain an artist once he grows up.

Pablo Picasso

Several years ago, I was a young therapist starting out at my first job running day-treatment programs at a local community mental health center. I had just completed my master's degree in counseling. I was a good student and I felt prepared by the graduate program that included courses in group therapy, counseling theory, and counseling children. I was excited and ready for the real world. Or so I thought.

I learned very quickly that while the academic knowledge is essential for mental-health professionals, there is no substitute for experience. When I arrived for my first day of work to run the two-hour day-treatment program for children with behavior problems, I realized I had no idea what to do or what kind of activities would work. After spending several days crying and thinking I had chosen the wrong profession, I got busy. I searched the internet and bought as many books as I could find on working with children. Many of these books contained good handouts and topics to discuss. With the help of those books and a good behavior plan, I made it through my first several months of the real world.

As time went on, I discovered that while the therapeutic worksheets and handouts from the resource books provided something for the children to do and the behavior plan helped to manage their behavior, they did not seem excited about the group. I slowly began to venture outside the box and try to put a therapeutic spin on creative activities. As I become more and more comfortable using these activities, I found the participants in my group to be more excited about coming to group. Attendance and behavior began to improve. Art and other creativity methods seemed to be natural forms of expression for children.

Later, I accepted a position supervising all of the day-treatment programs at the community mental health center. I had the opportunity to work with children aged 2 to 18, and learn from many of the other therapists at the center. My knowledge of creativity therapy increased and I encouraged other therapists to implement more expressive arts and creativity into the programs. I also learned a lot from many of the other therapists working at the center about creative counseling. While supervising these programs, I coordinated and implemented many of the activities described in this book.

I recently accepted a position in our local school system working with children. Most school counselors do not have as much time to spend with children as therapists in an outpatient setting. As a result of this experience, I have developed and included brief activities that would be appropriate for these settings. There are also many ideas that would be helpful in classroom guidance situations. Most of the activities are cost-effective and easy to do.

The book is organized into five chapters to assist in quickly locating the type of activity needed. The first chapter includes icebreaker activities that can be used to begin individual and group counseling sessions and build rapport with children and teens. Many of these icebreakers would also work well with adults. The second chapter includes bibliotherapy (using books, poetry, and other forms of literature as part of counseling or therapy) and cinematherapy (using movies or television shows as part of counseling or therapy) activities. The bibliotherapy activities that accompany several children's storybooks would work well with elementary-school-aged children. The cinematherapy activities are appropriate for use with upper middle school and high-school-aged adolescents. These activities would also work well with adults. The third chapter includes a variety of art therapy activities. These activities focus on the development of social skills, conflict-resolution skills, positive-thinking skills, and many other important therapeutic skills through a variety of modalities including painting, interactive activities, creative writing, and beading. The fourth chapter focuses on ideas to use for monthly character education topics. The activities for each month coordinate with some of the common themes and associations of the month. For example, February includes therapeutic activities associated with Valentine's Day, July includes ideas for Summer Sand Castle Building, and August has ideas for Back to School Events. The final chapter includes ideas for conducting therapeutic day camps. This section offers topic ideas for the camps, activity descriptions, sample schedules, and handouts. It also provides ideas for making the camp activities work in other settings.

Most of the activities in this book are applicable to a range of different settings (schools, community agencies, day care centers, etc.) and will work with a wide range of ages, from early elementary school to adults. These resources and activities can be adapted for individual or group sessions. Some of the activities can be completed quickly within a single group session, while others could be completed over several sessions as a unit or area of focus for several sessions. Based on the needs of the child and group, many of the activities are flexible and can be modified for use with different type of groups and within the amount of time available. Please be creative and feel free to make any needed adjustments so that the activities will work for the children and teens in your setting.

When first introducing some of these activities, you may encounter some resistance (especially from adolescents) to participating and completing the activity. While it is beyond the scope of this book to completely address the issue of resistance, there are a few things you can do to engage children and adolescents and encourage them to participate. Begin by presenting activities in a non-threatening way. Let the participants know that they do not have to share their artwork with the group unless they choose to do so. If adolescents know that they will not be "put on the spot," they may be more likely to participate and give the activity a chance. Remind them that they are not being judged or graded on their final product. Instead, it is the process that is the important part. Give the participants some choice and autonomy in completing the project. Try not to use a "one size fits all" approach or correct participants who are not completing the activity exactly as it is designed. By allowing the participant to choose what materials to use and how to design his or her project, you may learn of a better or more unique way of doing things. Participate and complete the activity along with the group. If the children and adolescents see that you are willing to do what you are asking them to do, they may be more likely to participate. Clearly when working with young children and teenagers it is important to ensure that none of the materials used with them contain swearing, profanity, inappropriate sexual references, excessive violence, or any references to ideas beyond their understanding. So it is important to always check that any books, videos, or DVDs that you intend to use with your groups are appropriate to their age and understanding.

The use of a basic behavior plan may help in getting started with the group and with some of the activities in the group. Allow students to earn points for displaying a good attitude, participating in the group, and attempting the project. These points can be exchanged for a special snack or reward at the end of the group time. As the group becomes more and more willing to participate, these rewards can be faded out. If one student is unwilling to participate, go ahead and complete the activity with the rest of the group. Ignore this child's behavior while making the activity as fun and engaging as possible for the rest of the group. After watching the fun everyone else is having, the child may become more willing to participate. Remember to remain positive and provide consistent praise to the participants who are engaged in the activity.

At times, some of the activities may bring up difficult feelings or emotions for the participants. It is important to discuss this with group members at the beginning of the group session. Confidentiality is a critical issue for groups. Complete an informed-consent process with the group explaining the group rules, the expectations, confidentiality and limits of confidentiality, as well as other pertinent information during the first session of the group. Let group members know that keeping private the information discussed in group is a key to the success of the group. Explain that you will keep all information discussed confidential, but you cannot guarantee that other group members will do so. Remind members frequently about the importance of confidentiality and trust within the group. Be sure to watch for conflicts and issues within the group and discuss these in an open and honest way with the group as soon as they arise, to prevent them from impacting the unity of the group. If a group member is struggling with a particular issue or painful emotion, you may have to use your best judgment about how to address the concern. At times, the staff members and other participants can provide feedback and help the participants process the feelings within the group setting. However, some issues that come up (abuse, neglect, trauma, etc.) may not be appropriate for addressing within the group setting. The staff member will need to communicate with the participant's parent or guardian and consider a referral to more intensive counseling services. Consult with a colleague or supervisor and consult ethical guidelines if you are unsure how to handle a difficult situation within the group setting.

My hope is that you will find this book helpful. It is a book I wish had been available when I first started in the mental-health field. It is a collection of activities that I have gathered from personal experience and from watching and learning from mentors and colleagues. The activities have served me well as I have counseled children and teens in a variety of settings. My primary goal for the book is to assist you in making the counseling process not only productive and therapeutic, but also fun and engaging for children and teens. I hope the activities and resources assist in making working with children and teens an exciting, creative, and rewarding experience for you and your clients. Thank you for choosing this book. I hope that it serves you well in your work with children and teens.

CHAPTER 1

Opening Activities
Warm-Ups, Icebreakers, and Other Brief Activities

Begin at the beginning...and go on till you come to the end: then stop.

Lewis Carroll, *Adventures in Wonderland*

Icebreakers do exactly what they sound like they do—they put both the child and you at ease so that productive work can take place. Many of these activities can provide a lot of information while making the child comfortable with you as the counselor and the counseling process.

PICTURE PROMPTS

Materials needed

- Card

- Old magazines (home magazines, women's magazines, and magazines about family life are great sources…especially the advertisements)

- Glue

Purpose of the activity

- To put the child/adolescent at ease

- To introduce self to counselor or group in a non-threatening way

- To provide a prompt for further self-exploration

- To stir the creative thought-process

- To involve uninterested or depressed adolescents in counseling (it does not require much effort)

Description of the activity

Using old magazines (which is a great way to recycle), cut out pictures of images and phrases that could foster memories or associations with others. The possibilities for such images are endless, but some examples include images of families on vacation, people sitting alone, and nature scenes. Glue these onto card, cut to the size of the pictures, and laminate if possible. Keep a basket with a variety of images. When the child or adolescent arrives, ask him or her to select an image that identifies how he or she is feeling. You can then ask him or her to verbally elaborate on that choice, journal about the image, or draw a response to the image. If journaling or drawing is chosen as a means of responding, then the counselor can process the response with the client when complete.

Variations of the activity

- Group Introductions—Ask each group member to select a picture and use the picture to introduce him- or herself to the group

- Picture Pair Share—Divide the group into pairs and give each pair an image. Ask everyone to think about a memory or association with the picture, and ask them to share their associations with their partners. When this is complete, ask them to introduce their partners to the group and tell them about their response to the picture.

- Now and Later—Ask the child to select a card that reminds him or her of how things are now and how he or she wants things to be later. Allow the child to draw, journal, or collage about the activity and then discuss with the child.

- Now and Then—Ask the adolescent to choose a card to represent how things are now and how things were in the past. Allow the child to draw, journal, or respond to the pictures and then discuss.

- Me As I Want To Be—Let the child select a card to represent how he or she wants to "be" in the future, discuss what steps the child would need to take to be like the picture, and allow the child to take the picture as a visual reminder of his or her goal.

- Behavior Reminder—For a child who has difficulty maintaining a certain behavior at school (such as staying in his or her seat), find a picture of a child of similar age and background exhibiting the behavior appropriately and tape the picture to his or her desk as a visual reminder.

- Picture This—Counselors can use this variation to provide encouragement to children. If an adolescent is close to meeting a goal (such as graduating from high school), the counselor could give the adolescent a picture of a graduate cap or diploma, and a short message or inspiring quote could be written on the back of the image. These are often very meaningful to clients. This could also be used after a goal has been reached, to "commemorate" the occasion.

- Calming Card—For children with anxiety or anger issues, assist them in selecting a picture of something soothing and calming to them (the beach, a dog, etc.). Discuss ways to self-soothe and relax. Let them take the picture as a reminder of how to calm down and focus when feeling anxious or upset.

INITIALLY YOURS

Materials needed

- Paper
- Markers

Purpose of the activity

- To begin the counseling session with an activity using familiar aspects of self
- To promote self-esteem and self-expression
- To build rapport between the counselor and child

Description of the activity

Most individuals are comfortable with their own names and initials. After all, we use them numerous times a day! Begin by giving the adolescents a sheet of paper and pack of markers (or other drawing materials). Ask them to write their initials on the paper and then turn them into a meaningful picture. Tell them that all of their initials can be used or just one initial. They can make the initials as big or small as they choose. Share with the group (if used in a group setting). See the above illustration for an example of this activity. Can you see the initials "LMJ" in the butterfly? (Hint: Check the wings and body!)

Variations of the activity

- ABC, Easy as 123—Complete the above activity but use the first initial of their name and the number of their birth month. For example, my name starts with L and I was born in June so I would use an "L" and a "6" to complete the activity.

- Name Game—Complete the above activity but use the participant's first name or last name.

- Block Letter Shape—Provide group members with large alphabet stencils. Have members cut out one or all of their initials and decorate as they choose. They can make designs or draw symbols of things that represent themselves.

- Designs for U—Provide pony beads (round, solid colored beads available at craft stores, or see the Resources section at the end of this book for websites that offer craft supplies), alphabet beads (also available at craft stores) and cord. Let the group make name jewelry (bracelets, anklets, necklaces, etc).

IT'S A DOG'S LIFE

Materials needed

- Paper

- Markers, crayons, pencils

- Pictures and descriptions of different breeds of dogs (visit www.nationalkennelclub.com for a large list/description of different dog breeds)

Purpose of the activity

- To build rapport in a fun, creative way

- To identify various aspects of personality

- To introduce self to the group and learn about other group members

Description of the activity

Most children love animals, especially dogs. Begin the activity by giving out paper, markers, and the descriptions of dogs (for example, "Labrador Retrievers are friendly, loyal, and hard workers"). If you are not familiar with the different aspects of each dog breed, you can look these up on a computer search engine. Ask each child to identify which type of dog he or she is most like and write or draw a picture depicting why he or she identifies with that particular dog breed. Share these with the group. This activity could also be completed on large banner paper and made into a mural.

Variations of the activity

- What Puts You in the Dog House?—Ask children to identify behaviors they exhibit that get them into trouble at home or school. Ask children to sketch a dog house and have them write or draw these behaviors inside the house.

- What Gets You a Bone?—Ask children to identify behaviors that get them praise and rewards. Ask children to draw a dog bone and write some of the positive behaviors that get them rewards on the inside of the bone. Discuss the differences in the behaviors and rewards/consequences.

- Dog Movie Therapy—There are numerous dog movies with therapeutic messages that can be viewed (as a whole or in segments) and discussed as a group. A few examples include *All Dogs Go to Heaven*, *Marley and Me*, and *Lady and the Tramp*.

- Puppy Love—Discuss different types of love with the group. Adapt the discussion for children or adolescents. With children, discuss different ways to show love to family, friends, and others. Provide an outline of a heart and have the child draw or collage ways to show love. With adolescents, discuss love in relationships, infatuation, and related topics. Provide them with the heart outline and ask them to make a collage of ways to show love to others or what love means to them.

- Dog Days Week—Devote a week to discussing dogs from a therapeutic perspective, complete the above activities, take a trip to an animal shelter and deliver dog treats, and any other activities you can think of.

- Different Animal—Choose a different animal (for example cats, birds, sea animals) and modify the above activities to fit this animal.

WHAT'S THE STORY?

Materials needed

- Brown paper bag full of different items such as tape, soap, socks, etc. (any items found around the house or school will work)

OR

- Brown paper bag full of words (be sure to include nouns, verbs, and adjectives)
- Paper
- Pencils, markers, crayons

Purpose of the activity

- To develop creative thinking and critical thinking skills
- To provide a fun beginning to the group
- To get to know other group members

Description of the activity

Distribute paper and pencils or art supplies. Explain to the group that they are going to create a poem or short story based on some items (or words, depending on which bag you use) pulled from a bag. Ask one of the participants to come, close his or her eyes, and pull a certain number of items out of the bag. Hold up the items (or call out the words) for all of the group members to see. Ask them to create a poem or story that includes all of these items (or words). Share the stories or poems with the group when complete.

Variations of the activity

- Individual Story Pull—Allow each child to pull their own items or words from the bag so that each poem or story is about different items.
- Draw the Story—Instead of writing a story or poem, ask them to draw a picture that includes all the items.
- Create a Hidden Picture—Many children love to do hidden picture searches. Ask them to make their own hidden pictures by drawing a picture and "hiding" the items pulled from the bag by drawing them somewhere in the picture.
- Pull a Shape—Have a bag of shapes in different colors. Pull a shape from the bag and ask participants to draw a picture entirely made up of that shape.

Creative forms of journaling

Journals are already widely used in therapeutic settings. In fact, when I ran day-treatment programs, I started each day with journals. Journals are a daily log or diary of an individual's feelings, experiences, and observations about his or her life. Journals can be used daily, every other day, weekly, or on an "as needed" basis (when the person feels like writing in it). Journals should be a private place in which a person can release feelings and express personal thoughts. Children and adolescents should not be forced to share from their journals. However, they can be encouraged to talk about an experience, paraphrase what they wrote, or share when they feel comfortable. Using the same form of journaling each day can quickly become routine so I often tried to use different types of journaling activities each day. Listed below are some of the journals I used.

GRATITUDE JOURNALS

Materials needed

- Notebooks
- Pens, pencils, or markers
- Thank-you notes (store-bought or handmade)

Purpose of the activity

- To identify and focus on the positive aspects of life
- To show gratitude to others in appropriate ways
- To develop self-esteem and self-expression skills

Description of the activity

Once a week (or as desired, but not daily as this will make it "routine" instead of "special"), distribute notebooks designated as gratitude journals. Ask children to identify three things that they are grateful for this week and write or draw about these things in their journal. Once a month or every few weeks, ask children to identify someone in their gratitude journal who has done something nice for them and either write them a note on a store-bought thank-you note or create a handmade thank-you note. Have children mail or deliver the thank-you note to the recipient.

ART JOURNALS

Materials needed

- Notebooks
- Art materials (old magazines, markers, glue, scissors, paint, etc.)

Purpose of the activity

- To develop creative thinking skills
- To learn to express feelings and thoughts in a variety of ways
- To teach coping skills

Description of the activity

Once a week (or as desired, but not daily as this will make it "routine" instead of "special"), distribute art journals and various art supplies and allow the children or adolescents to create art for journal time. You may give them a prompt or simply have them create whatever art they desire. Provide time to share with the group if desired.

UP DAY, DOWN DAY JOURNALS

Materials needed

- Card, typing paper
- 3-hole punch
- Yarn or string to bind journals
- Pens, pencils, markers, etc.

Purpose of activity

- To learn to handle "bad" days in an appropriate and healthy way
- To ventilate and express thoughts and feelings
- To develop coping skills and anger management

Description of the activity

This style of journaling was used in several day-treatment programs at the facility I worked at, and many of the children really liked this type of journal. To create the journals, each child would get two pieces of card. One piece will serve as the front cover for UP days (good days) and one piece will serve as the back cover for DOWN days (bad days). They can be decorated as the child chooses. Next, punch holes in the card and typing paper and tie together using yarn or string. Each day as the child comes in, he or she will get the journal and choose the side to journal on in order to write or draw about his or her day. After finishing, the child can share with the group and leave the bad day on the DOWN side. This helps children to develop coping skills and anger management. It also helps to look back at the journal and compare UP days to DOWN days. Most children have more good days than bad days. The journal helps to reinforce the need for a positive attitude and letting go of negativity.

JOURNAL JARS

Materials needed

- Notebooks
- Jar filled with quotes, questions, and prompts
- Pens, pencils, markers

Purpose of the activity

- To develop creativity and critical-thinking skills
- To develop healthy self-expression and self-esteem
- To develop appropriate social skills and listening skills

Description of the activity

The counselor will fill a jar with meaningful quotes, questions, and other journal prompts on small strips of paper. Each day, one of the adolescents will be asked to pull from the jar and read the quote or question on the strip of paper. All members of the group will then write or draw their response to the quote or question in their journal. When completed (about 15 minutes is usually enough), each group member could share his or her response with the group.

JOURNAL JAMS

Materials needed

- Journals
- CD player and music (avoid any swearing)
- Pens, pencils, markers

Purpose of the activity

- To learn to express self through a creative outlet
- To develop coping skills and social skills
- To ventilate feelings through journaling and listening to music

Description of the activity

The counselor will distribute journals to the group and then ask them to listen to the song playing. Try to select some popular songs and also some less familiar songs to expose adolescents to new types of music over the course of the time in which they use these journals. Start off with popular songs that the adolescent will relate to easily. Be careful to avoid music containing swearing or vulgarity. Play the song for the group and ask them to respond to the song in their journal. Ask the group members to share their responses with the group.

COVERED WITH LOVE JOURNALS

Materials needed

- Several different patterns of brightly colored fabric—approx. 3 feet (1 meter)
- Three-ring binders
- Ruled paper and typing paper
- Scissors
- Fabric glue (see Resources section)
- Yarn or ribbon

Purpose of the activity

- To create a personal journal/diary to be used outside of the therapeutic setting
- To develop healthy coping skills
- To create a "safe" place to ventilate thoughts and feelings

Description of the activity

Cut fabric to the correct size to cover the binder—about 15 inches (40 centimeters) of a 44/45 inch (110 centimeters) length for a standard 1 inch (2 centimeter), 3 ring binder. Give each child the opportunity to choose his or her fabric to cover the binder. After everyone has selected fabric, instruct the group to work slowly and carefully. Ask them to put a small amount of fabric glue on the binder and then press the fabric on top of it while slowly smoothing the fabric to remove any wrinkles or bubbles. Keep repeating this procedure until the whole binder is covered in fabric. Cut the ribbon to fit the binder and attach to serve as a bookmark. Once complete, fill the first section with ruled paper and the second section with typing paper. Explain to the children that this journal will be one they keep at home and do not share with others unless they choose to. They can write or draw in it whatever they choose—it will be their creation.

Circle time ideas

SIGN IN AND BEGIN

Materials needed

- Large piece of paper (taped to the wall)
- Markers

Purpose of the activity

- To develop routine and structure for the group
- To establish group unity
- To provide a record of the group experience

Description of the activity

At the first session (or whenever you begin to use this sign-in wall), explain to the participants that at the beginning of each meeting they will sign in on the wall as they arrive. They can write their names, a quote describing how they feel, or draw a symbol or picture. After everyone has arrived and signed in, the group members can make observations about others' signature or drawings and discuss them as a group. It is helpful to set ground rules for this activity and discuss these as a group, especially with adolescents (examples of ground rules include no swearing, no vulgar symbols, no gang signs, etc.). Encourage the adolescents to respect others and their contributions to the sign-in wall. Adolescents can be very sensitive and may shut down if they feel that others are disrespecting them or their contributions to the sign-in wall. Most teens really like this way of beginning group and checking in at each session. It also becomes a visual symbol of the group's connection. With groups that have changing members, this activity should be used carefully as confidentiality could be broken and new group members could feel alienated by a well-developed group sign-in mural.

STORIES AND SNACKS/CHIPS AND CHAPTERS/BOOKS AND BREAKFAST

Materials needed

- Book, short story, poem, or chapter with a therapeutic topic or message
- Food (based on the above slogan use either snacks, chips or breakfast)

Purpose of the activity

- To expose participants to a new form of relaxation and coping
- To promote enjoyment of reading
- To introduce a therapeutic discussion topic

Description of the activity

Many children are not frequently read to at home, but books can present a therapeutic topic in a way that discussion alone cannot. During circle time, distribute food (based on the slogan chosen above) and ask children to get comfortable and relaxed. Read them the chosen short story. Ask questions when the book is finished to check listening (give out stickers or small candy as a prize for answering the question). Next, discuss the book's message or lesson as a group. Often, a supplemental activity can be developed to go along with the book (see the Bibliotherapy section in Chapter 2 for ideas).

Variations of the activity

- Music Slogans—Complete the above activity with music instead of books (develop catchy slogans for this such Lunch and Lyrics, Songs and Snacks, or Music and Munchies).
- Movie Slogans—Complete the above activity with movies instead of books (develop catchy slogans for this such as Movie Clips and Chips, Cinema and Cookies, or Movies and Munchies).

"BEANIE BABY" BEGINNINGS

Materials needed

- Beanie Babies or other small stuffed animals

Purpose of the activity

- To put children at ease
- To help children verbalize feelings more easily
- To develop social skills and communication skills

Description of the activity

This is a great use for Beanie Babies and works well with younger children. Keep an assortment of Beanie Babies in a basket or container. At the beginning, ask all the children to pick one of the Beanie Babies to represent themselves. Tell them to name their Beanie Baby and think about how the Beanie Baby is feeling today. Go around the group and get each child to tell the name of his or her Beanie Baby and how the Beanie Baby is feeling. Ask any questions directly to the Beanie Baby and have the child respond for it. At the end of Circle Time, return the Beanie Babies to the container to take a nap.

Variations of the activity

- Beanie Family—In individual sessions, let children pick Beanie Babies to represent members of their family and friends. Discuss why particular ones were chosen to represent certain family members (for example, "Grandmother is a bear with a heart on the chest because she loves me;" "Dad is a lion because he is loud and mean").

- Create a Beanie Story—Ask the child to pick a Beanie Baby (or Babies) and make up a story about the Baby. Discuss and process.

CHAPTER 2

Cinematherapy and Bibliotherapy Activities

There is creative reading as well as creative writing.

Ralph Waldo Emerson

Cinematherapy activities

THE BLIND SIDE

Materials needed

- DVD of *The Blind Side* movie (Warner Brothers, 2009)
- Access to a DVD player and a TV
- Paper (colored construction paper and white paper)
- Pencils, markers, crayons

Purpose of the activity

- To promote positive thinking and self-confidence
- To express gratitude and appreciation to others for support
- To learn to release negativity and hurtful words

Plot summary

The Blind Side is based on the true story of Michael Oher. The movie looks at how Michael, an underprivileged Memphis, Tennessee teenager, came to be part of a wealthy family and how then, as a result of his extraordinary talent, hard work, and the help of his family, he became a pro football player in the American NFL (National Football League). The movie provides an opportunity for groups to discuss overcoming negativity, family issues (including what defines a family), the importance of hard work and support from others, and issues relating to differences in socioeconomic backgrounds, race, and culture.

Description of the activity

As a group, view the movie *The Blind Side*. After viewing the movie, ask all participants to journal about their thoughts, feelings, and questions concerning the movie. Discuss as a group.

Sample discussion questions

- Would Michael's story be different if he was not so extraordinarily talented in football? Why?
- What do you think would have happened to Michael if he had not attended the private school or met the Tuohys?
- Who benefited more from Michael going to live with the Tuohys—Michael or the Tuohys? Why?
- What do you think about the accusations that the Tuohys only helped Michael because of his football talent?

- What obstacles did Michael have to overcome to get where he is today? What characteristics and traits did he have to develop along the way?

- Who was the most important member of Michael's support team? What did this person do to encourage and help Michael?

- What would Michael's life have been like if he had not been able to let go of anger and resentment about his childhood?

- What stereotypes do you see in the movie? Are these stereotypes accurate depictions of reality?

- How could you relate to Michael's story?

- Who are you grateful to in your own life for encouraging you and believing in you?

- What obstacles and negativity have existed or currently exist in your life? How did you overcome the obstacle or let go of the negativity or how do you plan to overcome the obstacle or let go of the negativity?

Variations of the activity

- Thank You for Believing in ME—Ask all participants to think of someone who has encouraged, supported, and believed in them and write a thank-you note to that person (store-bought or handmade). Deliver to the person if possible.

- Overcoming Obstacles and Negativity—Ask all participants to draw or write about what the obstacles and negativity in their lives look like and how they make them feel. Next, ask the participants to write or draw a picture of themselves overcoming the obstacle or negativity and reflecting belief in themselves. Discuss the responses as a group.

LEGALLY BLONDE

Materials needed

- DVD of *Legally Blonde* movie (MGM, 2001)
- Access to DVD player and a TV
- Access to a video camera
- Typing paper
- Markers
- Pencils
- Scissors
- Glue
- Old magazines

Purpose of the activity

- To encourage self-awareness and self-acceptance
- To understand the importance of hard work, goal setting, and perseverance
- To develop self-confidence and belief in overcoming obstacles and difficult circumstances

Plot summary

Legally Blonde tells the story of Elle Woods, a popular Californian girl, whose biggest concern is what to wear on her date with her boyfriend who she believes is going to propose to her. When he breaks up with her because he is going to Harvard Law School and doesn't think she is clever enough to be with him, Elle decides that she will show him. She applies to Harvard Law School and is accepted. Elle is far from the traditional Harvard student and must overcome several obstacles on her way to achieving her goal. Through hard work, dedication, and encouragement from her friends she becomes the valedictorian (highest achiever) of her class while still remaining true to herself. The movie provides groups with an opportunity to discuss issues related to overcoming obstacles, celebrating individuality, believing in yourself when others may not, showing kindness to others, and pursuing goals and dreams.

Description of the activity

As a group, view the movie *Legally Blonde*. After viewing the movie, ask each participant to journal about thoughts, feelings, questions, and reactions to the movie. Discuss as a group.

Sample discussion questions

- Compare Elle at the beginning of the movie to Elle at the end of the movie. What is the same about Elle? What has changed about Elle?
- How did Elle's goals and motivation for achieving her goals change throughout the movie?
- Assumptions and first impressions play a big role in the relationship between Elle and Vivian, her ex-boyfriend's new girlfriend. How have your first impressions or assumptions about others been correct or incorrect in the past? How have other people's first impressions or assumptions about you been correct or incorrect in the past?

- What obstacles and circumstances did Elle have to overcome to achieve her goals?

- Elle is not your typical Harvard law student. Have you ever been in a situation when you felt out of place or like you didn't belong? How did you handle it? Did the movie give you any ideas for handling situations where you feel out of place in the future?

- At the beginning of the movie, Elle is dependent on her boyfriend and her identity seems to be somewhat based on being his girlfriend. How do you feel about this? Can you relate? What happens when our identity and self-worth are connected to our relationships with others and their opinions of us?

- What do you find as the most encouraging or inspiring part of the movie? What lessons do you take from viewing the movie and discussing it?

Variations of the activity

- Admission Application—Ask each participant to create an admission application for the college or other program of his or her choice. The application should include an essay describing his or her strengths, goals for the future, unique qualities, and why the individual feels he or she is a good fit for the college. The application should also include a 2–3 minute oral presentation summarizing the information in the essay and the individual's personality. Encourage participants to be creative. If possible, videotape the presentations and view and discuss them as a group.

- Unlikely Friendships—Elle has several friendships with "unlikely" people who do not seem to have much in common with her. Think about your friendships. Write a poem or make a collage about what makes a good friend. What are the characteristics of a good friendship? How important is it to have things in common?

- True Values—Spend some time reflecting on the traits and characteristics of your personality that you are unwilling to change for any other person or opportunity. Write a brief life-mission statement to reflect these non-negotiable aspects of self and current goals. Share these with the group if desired.

THE WIZARD OF OZ

Materials needed

- DVD of *The Wizard of Oz* movie (MGM, 1939)
- Access to DVD player and a TV
- Enough copies of the Home Handout for all group members
- Paper

- Mural paper
- Pencils
- Markers
- Old magazines
- Glue
- Scissors

Purpose of the activity

- To discuss goals and the decision-making process
- To develop self-awareness and self-confidence
- To understand the importance of dealing with problems instead of avoiding them

Plot summary

The Wizard of Oz tells the story of Dorothy and her dog, Toto, who are transported from Kansas to the Land of Oz by a tornado. Dorothy begins to follow the yellow brick road to try to meet the Wizard of Oz because she believes he can send her home to Kansas. Along the way, Dorothy meets several friends including the Cowardly Lion, the Tin Man, and the Scarecrow. Dorothy's friends also want to see the Wizard of Oz because they believe he can provide them with things they are missing (courage for the Lion, a heart for the Tin Man, and a brain for the Scarecrow). As they continue on their journey and overcome enemies and challenges along the way, they finally reach the Wizard of Oz but soon discover they each had what they were looking for all along. The movie provides groups with an opportunity to discuss issues relating to friendships, searching for things from others, inner strength and fulfillment, overcoming challenges, and the importance of home (as well as what defines a home).

Description of the activity

As a group, view *The Wizard of Oz* movie. After the movie is over, ask participants to journal about their thoughts, feelings, questions, and reactions concerning the movie. Discuss the responses as a group.

Sample discussion questions

- Dorothy started out running from a problem (her neighbor trying to hurt her dog) and ends up with bigger problems (in a land far away from home). Have you started out trying to avoid one problem and ended up with bigger and more serious problems? What happened?

- Each of the characters in the movie already has what they are searching for, but does not believe it. Have you ever gone looking for or become obsessed with finding something that you already had?

- Dorothy and her friends think the Wizard can help them find the things they are looking for, but the Wizard turns out to be just a man. Have you ever put all your hope or belief in another person to only be let down? What happened? Discuss the issue of connectedness with others versus unhealthy dependence.

- Who was your favorite character in the movie? What did you relate to about the character?

- Dorothy is trying to get home to Kansas in the movie. Discuss the topic of home. Is home a place? Is home the people that live there? What is each person's personal definition of home?

- At the end of the movie, Dorothy and her friends all achieved their goals and found what they were looking for in Oz. What obstacles did they face in reaching their goals? How did they make decisions about what to do next? Despite the obstacles, do you think they felt the end result was worth it?

Variations of the activity

- Yellow Brick Road Mural—This activity can be completed individually or as a group. Give each person/group a large piece of mural paper, and paint or markers. Ask them to create their own yellow brick road mural depicting their journey toward their goals. They can use symbols or short phrases to depict challenges, obstacles, high points, significant events, and their goals along the road. Encourage them to be creative and have fun. Share with the group when complete.

- "No Place Like Home" Collage—Distribute copies of the Home Handout, glue, scissors, and old magazines. Ask group members to make a collage about what home means to them inside the Home template on the handout. If desired, they can cut the home out when complete. Share and discuss with the group.

- Symbol of Achievement—Even though the Wizard does not have the power to give each character what he or she desires (because they already have it!), he does give each character a tangible symbol (a diploma for the Scarecrow, a medal of valor for the Lion, and a heart-shaped watch for the Tin Man). Create your own tangible symbol as a reminder of a goal you worked hard for and achieved. Allow participants to use various art methods to create their symbols (drawing, painting, collage, modeling clay, writing poem or song, etc.). Share results with the group.

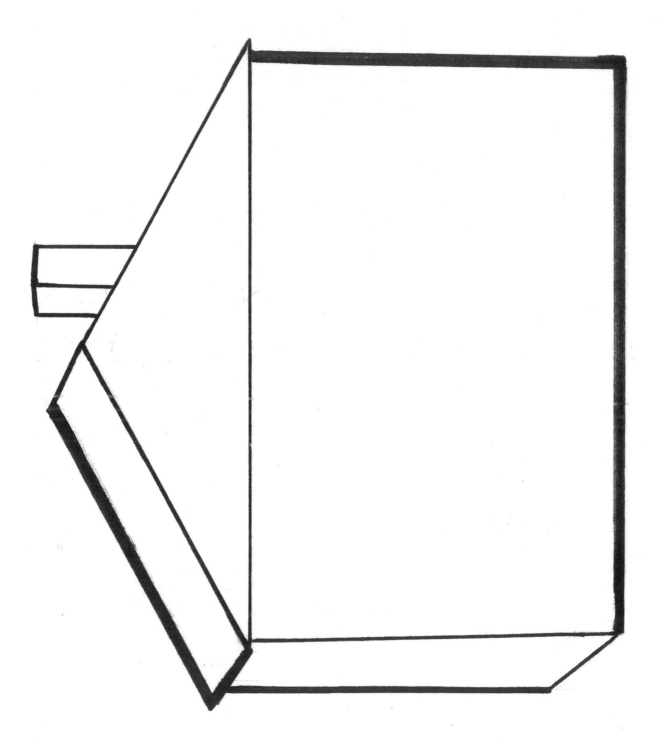

A RAISIN IN THE SUN BY LORRAINE HANSBERRY

Materials needed

- DVD of *A Raisin in the Sun* movie (Sony Pictures, 2008)
- Access to DVD player and a TV
- Copies of the play *A Raisin in the Sun* (obtain from online book retailers)

- Paper
- Markers, pens, pencils
- Old magazines
- Scissors
- Glue

Purpose of the activity

- To discuss and understand the importance of hope and positive thinking
- To understand and discuss family roles and relationships
- To express dreams and ways to deal with delayed progress and rejection

Plot summary

A Raisin in the Sun tells the story of the Younger family. The Youngers are a working-class African-American family living in Chicago, Illinois, in the 1950s. The Youngers are about to receive a payment from the life insurance policy for the deceased Mr. Younger. Each of the adult Youngers would like to spend the money in a different way. Mrs. Younger (the grandmother and wife of the deceased Mr. Younger) would like to buy a home for the family, Beneatha (Mrs. Younger's daughter) would like to use the money for her medical school tuition, and Walter Lee (Mrs. Younger's son) would like to use the money to buy a liquor store with a friend. As the Younger family tries to decide what to do, the bonds of family are tested, but the family comes out stronger and more united at the end. The movie allows groups to discuss family roles, dealing with conflicts and disagreements, overcoming racism and discrimination, dealing with delays and lack of progress, and the importance of hope in the face of adversity.

Description of the activity

As a group, view the movie *A Raisin in the Sun*. After viewing the movie, give group members some time to reflect on the movie and journal about thoughts, reactions, questions, or feelings concerning the movie. Discuss as a group.

Sample discussion questions

- Each family member has a different idea of what to do with the money based on his or her dreams. Have you ever been in a situation where your goals and dreams conflicted with the goals and dreams of someone close to you?
- Which character did you most identify with? Why?

- Which character did you least identify with? Why?

- There are several unresolved issues at the end of the movie/play (such as what Beneatha will do and how the family will make it in their new life outside the apartment). What do you think the future holds for each member of the Younger family?

- Walter trusted his friend, Willy, with his money and his dream, but he was betrayed. Have you ever been in a similar situation? How did you respond?

- Even though the family frequently disagrees and has many conflicts, they come together to support each other when it really matters. How do you feel about family? What is most important about family to you? What defines family?

Variations of the activity

- Hope and Dreams Collage—Ask adolescents to make a collage about hope and then write a short written response to accompany the collage. Share and discuss as a group.

- Read through the play of *A Raisin in the Sun* as a group. Discuss each character and his or her dreams, struggles, and hopes. Who does each group member most identify with?

- Create a new metaphor (instead of a raisin in the sun) for a dream deferred. Draw the metaphor. Share and discuss the metaphors as a group.

- Family Matters—Draw and design the family's new home. How do you see the family living together in their new home? What does the future hold for each family member? Briefly answer the questions and attach to the home design. Share and discuss with the group.

MEAN GIRLS

Materials needed

- Copy of *Mean Girls* DVD (Paramount Pictures, 2004)
- Access to DVD player and a TV
- Paper
- Pencils, markers

- Old magazines
- Scissors
- Glue
- Mural paper

Purpose of the activity

- To understand the importance of being yourself
- To understand the need to treat others with respect and kindness
- To develop empathy and social skills

Plot summary

Mean Girls tells the story of Cady Heron, a teenager who has been raised in Africa but at 15 enrolls in a high school in the United States. Through the course of the movie, Cady becomes friends with several different groups (including some who do not have her best interests at heart) and has to deal with the reactions of her "friends" when she begins to date one of their ex-boyfriends. While she makes some mistakes along the way, Cady comes out stronger and better at the conclusion of the movie. The movie will give groups the opportunity to discuss what makes a "real" friend, how to learn from mistakes, appreciating diversity and individuality, the challenges that face teens in high schools today, and how to deal with those who are mean and unkind to others.

Description of the activity

As a group, view the movie *Mean Girls*. After viewing the movie, give each participant time to reflect on the movie and journal about any thoughts, feelings, or questions. Discuss as a group.

Sample discussion questions

- Are the Plastics an accurate depiction of popular students in your high school? How do people get to be popular? Who determines what is popular? What does popular mean?
- What changes do you see in Cady throughout the movie? How does she lose her individuality and become like the Plastics? What do you think about Cady at the end of the movie?
- Why do you think Regina is so mean to others? What would motivate her to keep the burn book? How do you think Regina feels about herself?

- Are the Plastics really friends to each other? Why do you think they choose to spend time with each other? What makes a real friend? Is it important to be able to be yourself with your friends? Why?

- What did you think about Cady being crowned Spring Fling Queen and then breaking her tiara and giving the pieces to her classmates? What was the symbolism of the gesture?

- Discuss the issue of respect for others. How do you treat others with respect?

- What do you think is the message or theme of the movie? What did you take away from watching it?

- Is the movie a realistic portrayal of high school today? What parts did you relate to? What parts did you not relate to?

Variations of the activity

- The Kindness Book—Instead of "The Burn Book," create "The Kindness Book" as a group. Give each group member a piece of white paper. Ask each member to personalize the page by putting his or her name on it, as well as any other information you think is useful. Pass the pages around the group and allow other group members to write positive things (good character traits, ways the person has been kind to others, positive changes observed in the person, etc.) about the person on the page. When complete, compile all the pages into a book to keep in the group room. Make each person a copy of his or her page. In order to protect confidentiality do not make each person a copy of the whole book (if used in a therapeutic setting).

- Individuality Collages—Distribute old magazines, scissors, glue, and paper to make collages. Ask participants to make a collage about their individual personality and the things about themselves that they would not change to please others. Share and discuss with the group.

- "Pieces of Us" Mural—Draw a large tiara on a piece of mural paper. Give the participants markers, scissors, glue, and old magazines. Ask them to discuss Cady breaking the tiara at the Spring Fling and giving the pieces to her classmates. Ask each of them to think of something positive that they contribute to the group—their piece. Ask each person to draw or find pictures in the magazines to represent the positive piece he or she brings to the group. Discuss when complete.

Bibliotherapy activities

IF BY RUDYARD KIPLING

If you can keep your head when all about you
Are losing theirs and blaming it on you,
If you can trust yourself when all men doubt you,
But make allowance for their doubting too;
If you can wait and not be tired by waiting,
Or being lied about, don't deal in lies,
Or being hated, don't give way to hating,
And yet don't look too good, nor talk too wise:

If you can dream—and not make dreams your master;
If you can think—and not make thoughts your aim;
If you can meet with Triumph and Disaster
And treat those two impostors just the same;
If you can bear to hear the truth you've spoken
Twisted by knaves to make a trap for fools,
Or watch the things you gave your life to, broken,
And stoop and build 'em up with worn-out tools:

If you can make one heap of all your winnings
And risk it on one turn of pitch-and-toss,
And lose, and start again at your beginnings
And never breathe a word about your loss;
If you can force your heart and nerve and sinew
To serve your turn long after they are gone,
And so hold on when there is nothing in you
Except the Will which says to them: "Hold on!"

If you can talk with crowds and keep your virtue,
Or walk with Kings—nor lose the common touch,
If neither foes nor loving friends can hurt you,
If all men count with you, but none too much;
If you can fill the unforgiving minute
With sixty seconds' worth of distance run,
Yours is the Earth and everything that's in it,
And—which is more—you'll be a Man, my son!

Materials needed

- Enough copies of the poem *If*
- Old magazines
- Scissors
- Glue

- Paper
- Pens, markers
- Enough copies of the Pie Handout (see the *Enemy Pie* activity)

Purpose of the activity

- To discuss the importance of good character and morals
- To discuss being authentic and sincere with all people
- To understand the difference between pride and humility

Description of the activity

Distribute copies of the poem *If* and read it aloud as a group. Allow the group to reflect on the poem. Give out supplies and ask participants to fold a piece of paper in half. On one side, ask them to draw, collage, or write about the person they present to the world. On the other side, ask them to draw, collage, or journal about the person they are on the inside. Discuss the two sides and ask each person to identify ways to make the two sides match.

Variations of the activity

- Modern Translation—Ask the group members to rewrite the poem in words that make sense to them and/or to include situations or examples that reflect the poem's meaning. Share these with the group.

- Important People—Many people treat "kings" (discuss what the author means by king in the poem, i.e. powerful people, popular people, etc.) better than they treat other people. Discuss traits that really make people important (kindness, generosity, etc.). Ask group members to think of one person that the world would not consider "important," but who is important to them and get them to journal about this person.

- Humble Pie—Give each person a Pie Handout (see the *Enemy Pie* activity) and ask them to write something they are proud of on each slice of the pie (an accomplishment, physical trait, etc.). Pies are made to be shared and given away piece by piece. Ask each person to determine a way to "give away" each of the things they are proud of on their pie. (Examples of this might be a good football player who spends time with younger children teaching them to play football or a girl who is proud of her pretty hair and helps others style their hair.) Discuss with the group what happens to a pie that does not get eaten (spoils), and explain how it is the same with things we have received or accomplished—if they are not shared then they can make us "spoil." Eat pie as a group if possible!

ALEXANDER AND THE TERRIBLE, HORRIBLE, NO GOOD, VERY BAD DAY BY JUDITH VIORST

Materials needed

- A copy of *Alexander and the Terrible, Horrible, No Good, Very Bad Day*
- Markers, pencils
- Paper
- Old magazines
- Scissors
- Glue
- Enough copies of the Day Schedule Handout

Purpose of the activity

- To develop positive-thinking skills
- To identify ways to turn "negative" events into "positive" events
- To recognize ways to enjoy self and engage in pleasurable activities

Plot summary

This children's book tells the story of Alexander, who is having a very bad day. All kinds of things go wrong in Alexander's day including not getting a prize in his cereal, having to buy plain sneakers, and getting a cavity in his teeth. Children will be able to relate easily to many of the situations described in the book. The book helps children to understand that some days things just do not happen in the way that we would like them to happen, but there is always another day. The book provides the opportunity to discuss positive thinking with children, as well as the idea of accepting that sometimes things are not going to go our way.

Description of the activity

Many children tend to focus on the negative things that happen or let one thing ruin their day. Read the book together. After the book is finished, ask questions to ensure listening and comprehension (offer small candy or stickers for correct answers). Next, ask the children to draw a picture or make a collage and plan their perfect day. If desired, use the Day Schedule Handout. After everyone is finished, discuss as a group.

Variations of the activity

- Turn it Around—List all the "bad" things that happened to Alexander on a poster-board. As a group, discuss what he could think or do to turn each event from a "bad" event to a "good event." Also discuss that some days are just not as good as others, in order to help children develop realistic expectations along with positive thinking.

- Divide the group in half. Ask one group to make an argument stating that the reason Alexander's day was bad was because of the events that happened. Ask the other group to make an argument that the reason Alexander's day was bad was because of his attitude.

Have both sides present their argument and then decide as a group who was "right." (Hint: It was probably a little of both reasons.)

- Bad Day Book—Ask students to create a book (using drawings, writing, and/or collage) to cheer themselves up when they are having a bad day.

- In an individual session, read the book and ask the child to think about his or her worst day ever. Assist the child in going through it event by event, discussing it and, if possible, gaining perspective and a positive interpretation of the events.

Day Schedule Handout

7:00 a.m.	
8:00 a.m.	
9:00 a.m.	
10:00 a.m.	
11:00 a.m.	
12:00 p.m.	
1:00 p.m.	
2:00 p.m	
3:00 p.m.	
4:00 p.m.	
5:00 p.m.	
6:00 p.m.	
7:00 p.m.	
8:00 p.m.	
9:00 p.m.	
10:00 p.m.	
11:00 p.m.	
12:00 a.m.	

THE TRUE STORY OF THE THREE LITTLE PIGS BY JON SCIESZKA

Materials needed

- Copy of *The True Story of the Three Little Pigs*
- Paper
- Pencils, markers

Purpose of the activity

- To develop perspective/conflict-resolution skills
- To understand two viewpoints
- To develop social skills

Plot summary

Most children are familiar with the traditional story of *The Three Little Pigs* (visit the following website for a summary of the original version—http://storynory.com/2008/02/25/the-three-little-pigs-2). *The True Story of the Three Little Pigs* tells the story from the perspective of the wolf. The wolf claims he was misunderstood and he was only trying to borrow a cup of sugar to make a cake for his dear old granny's birthday. This book provides the opportunity to discuss different perspectives and viewpoints, telling the truth, and ways to resolve conflicts.

Description of the activity

Read the story as a group and ask the group questions to check for listening and comprehension (offer small prizes or candy). Explain to the group that you are going to have a trial for the wolf to determine if he is guilty. Arrange the room to look as much like a courtroom as possible. Assign group members to play all of the main characters of the book (the wolf, the pigs, the wolf's granny, the police), as well as members to serve as the judge, the lawyers (defense attorney and prosecutor) and the jurors. A script can be developed or group members can get into character and "ad lib" their parts. After the trial is complete and the wolf has received his verdict, ask the jurors what determined their verdict. Discuss perspective and the two sides of the story with the group.

Variations of the activity

- The True Story of…—Ask group members to take another common story or fairy tale and tell the "real" story (examples include *Goldilocks and the Three Bears*, *Snow White and the Seven Dwarfs*, and *Pinocchio*). Share the "true" story with the group.

- Ask group members to write a persuasive essay about whose story they believe—the wolf's or the pigs'. Ask them to include supporting details and evidence for their conclusion. Share them with the group and discuss both sides.

- Discuss perspective with the group. Often we only hear and believe one side of an issue. Had anyone ever thought before that there might be another version of *The Three Little Pigs*? How do they feel after they heard it? Did it change their perspective at all?

PURPLICIOUS BY VICTORIA KANN AND ELIZABETH KANN

Materials needed

- Copy of *Purplicious*
- Paper
- Markers
- Old magazines
- Pencils
- Enough copies of the Color Wheel Handout

Purpose of the activity

- To develop empathy and understanding of other's feelings
- To identify qualities of a good friend
- To develop self-concept and self-esteem

Plot summary

This children's book tells the story of Pinkalicious and Purplicious. Pinkalicious loves the color pink. She dresses all in pink and makes pink a part of everything she does until some other children at school tell her that "pink is out." Pinkalicous feels sad and depressed that others feel that way about her favorite color and she stops making pink a part of everything she does. But then, she meets Purplicious, whose favorite color is purple, and Pinkalicious understands that it is okay to be herself and love pink. This book provides the opportunity to discuss individuality, being kind to others, dealing with sadness, and friendship.

Description of the activity

Read the story to the group and ask questions to ensure listening and comprehension (offer small prizes). Pair up the children in groups of two. Ask them to think about the following questions:

- What were Pinkalicious' best traits?
- Why were the kids mean to Pinkalicious?
- How would you have felt if you were her?
- Do you ever treat others badly just because they are different?
- What kind of friend was Purplicious?
- How did she make Pinkalicious feel?

Ask each pair to write a poem, story, or create a collage about the friendship between Pinkalicious and Purplicious. Share these with the group.

Variations of the activity

- Color Wheel—Use this activity to talk about colors and the meanings we associate with colors (seeing red = angry, blue skies = calm, bright yellow = happy, etc.). Have each child create a color wheel (using drawings or magazine pictures) of the feelings and things he or she associates with each color. Use the Color Wheel Handout.

- Personal Color Wheel—Discuss favorite colors and how they reflect our personalities. Ask each child to think of words that describe him- or herself and then create a collage (from drawings or magazines pictures) using only his or her favorite color on the Color Wheel Handout. Ask the children to try to find pictures that reflect the descriptions of their personality. Share with the group.

✓

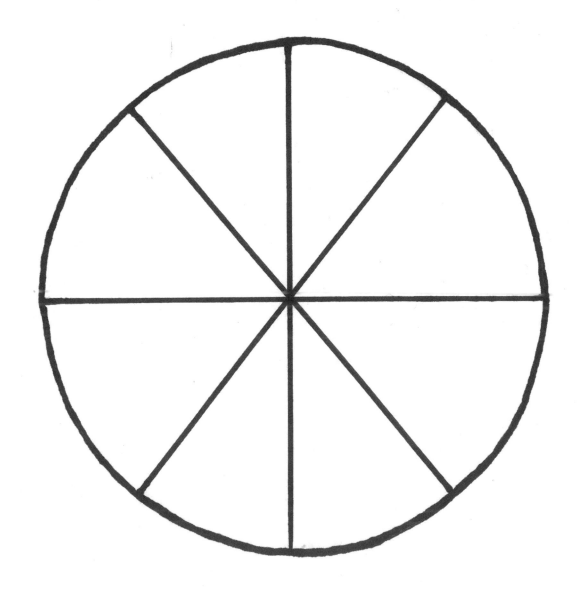

ENEMY PIE BY DEREK MUNSON

Materials needed

- A copy of *Enemy Pie*
- Trail mix materials (pretzels, nuts, raisins, potato chips, sunflower seeds, small chocolate candies, small cheese crackers, etc.)
- Airtight plastic bags
- Markers, pencils
- Enough copies of the Recipe Card Handout
- Pie Handout

Purpose of the activity

- To identify the qualities of a good friend
- To identify and understand healthy conflict-resolution skills
- To develop social skills and teamwork

Plot summary

This children's book tells the story of a boy who has an "enemy" on his street named Jeremy Ross. As the boy tells his dad about his enemy, his dad tells him that he has a recipe for enemy pie, but the pie will only work if he is kind to Jeremy before he eats it. The boy goes to play with Jeremy so that he will eat the pie. As it turns out, he has a great day with Jeremy and discovers they have a lot of things in common. When it comes time for the pie to be served, the boy is panicked because he does want his new friend to eat the pie, but then he realizes that his dad is eating the pie, too, and he has learned a valuable lesson. This book provides the opportunity to discuss friendships, social skills, conflict resolution, and accepting others.

Description of the activity

Read the story as a group and ask questions to ensure listening and comprehension (offer small prizes for correct answers). Discuss how the "enemies" became friends in the book. Pair the students up and give each pair a Recipe Card Handout and list of trail mix foods. Ask each pair to make a trail mix recipe for turning an enemy into a friend (for example, pretzels could stand for joining arms in friendship, small chocolate candies for being more and more patient with our friends, etc.). After each pair has completed their recipe, share it with the group. If time and resources allow, let the group members make the trail mix to eat in the group or take home with them but be sure first to check for any food allergies.

Variation of the activity

- Friendship Pie—Give each participant a Pie Handout. Ask him or her to write a way to turn an enemy into a friend on each pie slice. Discuss these as a group. If possible, eat pie as a snack in the group this day. If time and space allow, get participants to decorate their pies. Get a large piece of paper and put the words "Friendship Pies" on the top. Ask group members to cut out their pies and put them on the paper to be displayed.

Recipe Card Handout

Ingredient list:

Recipe instructions:

Pie Handout

RAINBOW FISH BY MARCUS PFISTER

Materials needed

- Copy of *Rainbow Fish*
- Enough copies of the Scale Handout
- Enough copies of the Heart Handout
- Markers
- Large fish outline drawn on paper, based on size of group
- Glitter
- Glue

Purpose of the activity

- To understand the importance of giving and generosity
- To develop social skills
- To identify reasons not to be greedy

Plot summary

This children's book tells the story of Rainbow Fish, the most beautiful fish in the ocean. Rainbow Fish has a special type of scale, but he does not want to share it with the other fish in the ocean. When the other fish begin to ignore Rainbow Fish because of his greed, Rainbow Fish has to make a decision about whether to share his special scale. This book provides the opportunity to discuss social skills, sharing and giving to others, and individuality.

Description of the activity

Read the story as a group and ask questions to make sure the group was listening and understood the story concepts (offer small candy or stickers for correct answers). Using the Fish Handout as guidance draw a large fish to go up on the wall. Give each child a Scale Handout to cut out and decorate using glitter, markers, and other materials (this is to represent the special scales that the Rainbow Fish had). Encourage children to make the scales as beautiful as possible. While children are working, discuss some of the things that they could give others—time, toys, love, kindness, etc. When the scales are complete, attach them to the large wall fish and let all the children admire how beautiful the fish has become. Next, give out the Heart Handout and ask the children to think of someone they want to encourage and write that person's name on the heart. Ask them to cut out the hearts and remove their scale from the fish and replace it with the heart. On the back of their scales, ask them to copy the following poem to give to the person they chose:

> This scale means something special to me
> And I choose to share my creation with you
> Sharing our love is the key
> To a happy friendship for me and you.

Now discuss as a group that even though the beautiful scales are "gone" from the fish, the fish is full of hearts of love because everyone is being kind and generous. Ask the group members to take their scales home and give them to their chosen person.

Fish Handout

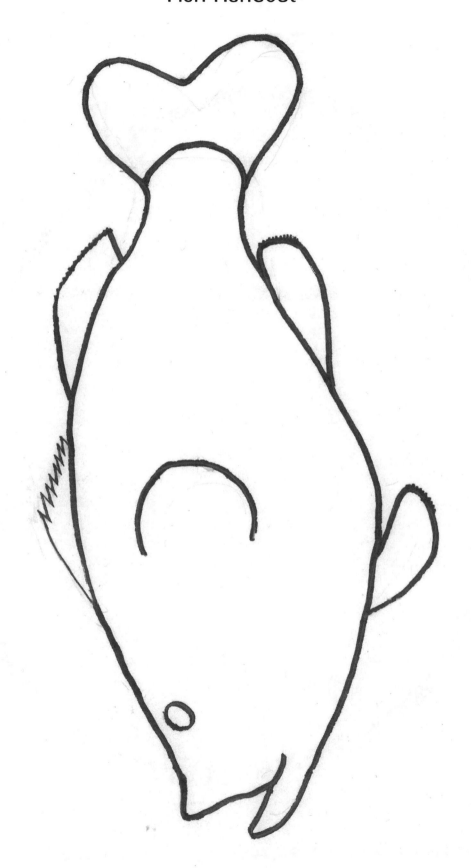

Scale Handout

Heart Handout

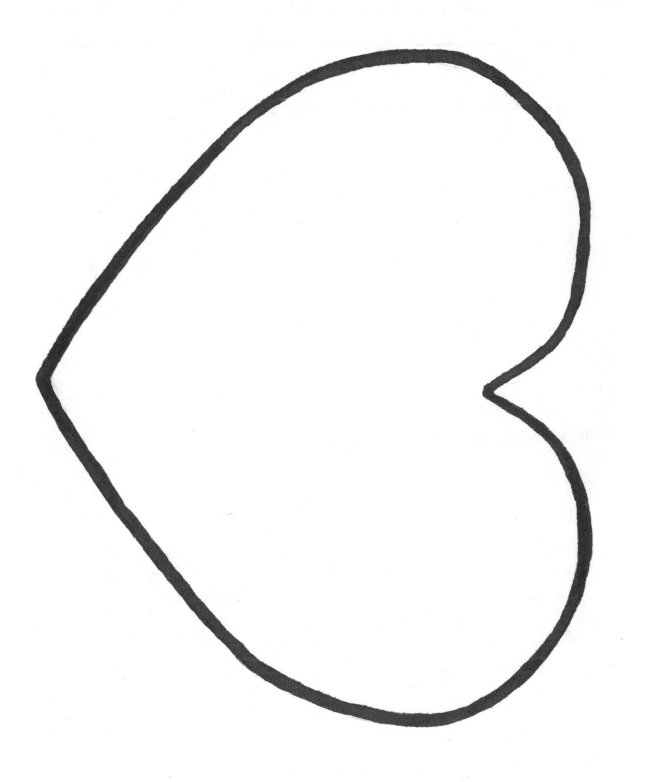

63

CHAPTER 3

Therapeutic Arts Activities

Art washes away from the soul the dust of everyday life.

Pablo Picasso

TIMELINE

Materials needed

- Blank paper
- Markers
- Other desired art supplies (collage materials, glitter, etc.)
- Enough copies of the Timeline Handout

Purpose of the activity

- To identify major incidents in life
- To discuss and process these events with therapists
- To reframe events when possible (discussing good things that came as a result of a bad event)

Description of the activity

This activity works well with adolescents (but most children are too young to appreciate the concept). Provide a copy of the Timeline Handout or give the individual a piece of blank paper (some people prefer to create their own timeline with ups and downs in the line). Ask the individual to reflect on his or her life and to create a visual timeline. Some suggestions to give the individual include creating a symbol for each important event and a symbol to indicate whether he or she considers that event to be good, bad, or neutral. Once the timeline is complete, discuss and process together by talking about the emotions associated with each event and the results (good and bad) of the event.

Variations of the activity

- Specific Timeline—Create specific timelines such as a School Timeline for school events, a Family History Timeline, or a Timeline of Moves for someone who has frequently moved to new places and experienced a lot of change. Timelines can also help the counselor and individual make sense of a lot of information and provide a starting point for counseling conversations.

- Mountains and Valleys—Another name for timelines. Ask individual to create a work of art reflecting the mountains and valleys in his or her life.

- A Chorus Line—Ask individual to create a mixed CD of songs that reflect different periods of his or her life. Ask each participant to choose one song (but screen these for inappropriate language/themes) to play for the group and discuss its meaning as a group.

- Journal Journeys—Assign a different phase of life each day (baby, early childhood, elementary, etc.) and ask participants to journal about this period. Combine together when all phases of life have been completed.

Timeline Handout

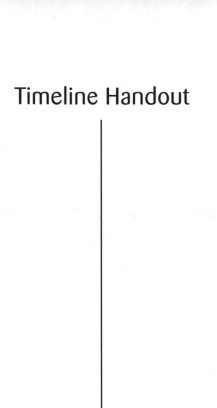

CITY OF HOPE

Materials needed

- Large piece of foam-board
- Cardboard pieces
- Construction paper
- Green towel or foam (for grass on city surface)

- Fabric glue
- Scissors
- Other desired art materials (glitter, paint, pipe cleaners, craft sticks, etc.)

Purpose of the activity

- To develop positive-thinking skills
- To see possibilities beyond current circumstances
- To develop social skills

Description of the activity

Many of the children I have worked with in the past have come from difficult neighborhoods and backgrounds. This activity helps them to see alternatives while using their creativity and working cooperatively together. Ask the group to think of their ideal community to live in. As a group, they can decide on the elements to include, such as a house for each group member, schools, playgrounds, churches, city hall, etc. The buildings can be made using cardboard and then painted and decorated as desired (see illustration above). This project can last several weeks and become a group project (I suggest working on it for 30 minutes a day over several weeks instead of trying to complete it in a day or two.) This project is only limited by the imagination. Children can look in magazines and cut out pictures of doors to use for their houses. They can name the town and buildings and elect a mayor and council members. They can create city laws. I have also seen groups include restaurants, soccer fields, and swimming pools (using Styrofoam bowls and cutting a hole in the board). This project could possibly be incorporated into a Social Studies class.

Variations of the activity

- Showcase of Cities—If several different groups or classes are making cities, have a showcase of cities and allow each group to tour the cities. If confidentiality is not an issue have each group give a presentation on their city and its special elements. Let them explain why their city is a city of hope.

- Progress Journals—Ask each group member to journal for five minutes daily about the city's construction and the difficulties and rewards of working with others. These will become a record of the experience when it is over.

MOSAIC MASCOTS

Materials needed

- Flat piece of artist canvas (16 x 20 inches/40 x 50 centimeters is a good size)
- Colored aquarium stones (these are cost-effective compared with other options)
- Fabric glue (See Resources section)

Purpose of the activity

- To develop patience and persistence
- To encourage a school spirit/organizational spirit
- To develop generosity and a giving attitude

Description of the activity

This is a great activity for participants to work on in pairs with supervision. It makes a great station in a group that uses centers or other areas where participants are working on different activities during the same time period. (In this context the term "station" means the site where a particular group activity will be carried out.) Before the project begins, ask someone with some artistic skill to draw the outline of the school mascot onto the canvas. It also helps if the canvas is color-coded using colored pencils to indicate which color stones go in which spot. Once this is complete, set up an area for participants to work on the mosaic. One way that works well is to spread a small amount of fabric glue onto the canvas and then press the aquarium stones onto the fabric glue. Once the project is complete, frame it if possible (inexpensive frames can be found at discount stores and craft stores) and allow students to donate it to their school (see illustration). If desired, the students can come up with a short presentation to do when donating the mosaic to the office staff.

Variations of the activity

- Mosaic Masterpieces—Complete the above activity but let the students choose a symbol to represent the group and create a mosaic of the symbol. Frame it and display in the group room.

- Charitable Creation—Pick a different organization (such as a hospital, community center, or nursing home) and create a mosaic to be donated there.

KNOCKING DOWN NEGATIVITY

Materials needed

- Cardboard boxes (of different sizes)
- Construction paper
- Markers
- Tape

Purpose the activity

- To identify negative influences and ways to minimize their effects
- To understand the importance of positive thinking
- To develop social skills and self-esteem

Description of the activity

Discuss as a group some of the things that keep us "stuck" in bad behavior (together with bad habits) and prevent us from achieving our goals or from trying something new. Examples include fear, anger, an unforgiving attitude, no motivation, complaining, low self-esteem, and many more. Divide the participants into smaller groups. Assign to each group one of the topics discussed. Have them write the topic on construction paper and place on one of the cardboard boxes. If desired, all the group members can write on small sheets of paper the ways that each of the topics has hurt them in the past and then put these inside the boxes. Tape the boxes shut. Now explain to the group that they are going to "knock down the negativity." Set the boxes up at one end of the room. For smaller children, you can let them go one at a time and knock down the boxes. For older children, the boxes can be set up and then they can "bowl" or use another non-aggressive method to knock down the boxes. After each group member has had a turn, discuss healthy ways to remove negativity or reduce its effects on our lives.

QUOTE QUESTS

Materials needed

- White card or paper
- Markers
- Old magazines
- Scissors
- Glue
- A book of famous quotes (or access to an internet site of famous quotes such as www.brainyquote.com) for creating a handout of your favorite quotes

Purpose of the activity

- To express oneself in a positive, creative manner
- To learn about self and others
- To promote positive group discussion

Description of the activity

I love quotes! This activity lets group members develop self-expression skills. Ask each group member to think of his or her favorite quote. Create and provide a handout with examples of your personal favorites (you can use the ones at the start of each chapter in this book if you wish) to give the participants some ideas. If participants are not sure of a favorite quote, let them look through the quote book or search the internet site for a personally meaningful quote. Once everyone has selected a quote, let the participants search magazines and collage about what the quote means to them. Share with the group and discuss each quote and collage.

Variation of the activity

- Quote Cues—Select a quote and have each group member make a collage about the quote's meaning to him or her. Share and discuss.

CRUSH THE CAN'TS, RAISE YOUR CANS[1]

Materials needed

- Two empty soda cans per participant
- Yarn/string
- Markers
- Construction paper
- Paper
- Glue or tape

Purpose of the activity

- To understand the importance of self-talk
- To become aware of personal negative self-talk and replace with positive statements
- To develop healthy self-esteem

Description of the activity

As a treat, have a soda party a few days before the activity to collect the cans for this activity. I often hear children saying "I can't do it," and this activity is a fun way to address this issue. Discuss and help children identify some of the things that they say "I can't" about. Fold the paper in half and have children draw a line down the page. Ask them to write some of these things on one side of the piece of paper and come up with symbols to represent them. Now help them to turn these "I can't" statements and symbols into "I can" statements and symbols. Have them write these on the other side of the piece of paper. Give each child two cans and two pieces of construction paper cut to the size of each can. Ask them to draw or write the "I can't" symbols and statements on one piece of the construction paper and the "I can" symbols and statements on the other. When completed, tape the "I can't" paper to one of the soda cans and the "I can" paper to the other soda can. Tell the children they are going to stomp out the "I can'ts." At the same time, have each child put his or her "I can't" can on the floor and rest a foot on top of it. Count to three and have everyone "crush the can'ts." Next, take a piece of yarn and string the "I can" cans through using the can top. Hang these in the group room to remind children to engage in positive self-talk.

---

1   This activity is adapted from an activity first learned about in a presentation by Dr. Joe Ray Underwood and Nancy Underwood at the Mississippi Counseling Association Annual Conference 2007.

COLOR CODING

Materials needed

- Enough copies of the Color Wheel Handout (see p.56)
- Old magazines
- Glue
- Scissors
- Markers

Purpose of the activity

- To identify and express feelings positively
- To develop self-concept and self-esteem
- To encourage creativity

Description of the activity

As a group discuss color meanings and the feelings we often associate with different colors. Discuss how a person's favorite color often becomes part of his or her identity. Listed below are some common color associations:

Red—Anger, love, fire

Blue—Calm, sadness, water

Green—Peace, intelligence, nature

Yellow—Happiness, energy, sunshine

Orange—Excitement, motivation, activity

Purple—Creative, unique, royalty

Black—Death, sophistication, darkness

White—Innocence, clean, pure

Give each participant a copy of the color wheel. Ask each of them to make a personal color wheel by drawing or selecting pictures that represent each color to him or her. Share with the group.

Variation of the activity

- Personal Color Code—Using the Color Wheel Handout, ask each participant to write his or her favorite color at the top and then in each of the color slots write words that are associated with the color and also describe him or her. Select pictures or draw pictures in each slot that are associated with the word and color. Share and discuss.

DREAM/GOAL BOARDS

Materials needed

- Foam-board or poster-board
- Old magazines
- Glue
- Scissors
- Markers

Purpose of the activity

- To understand the difference between goals and dreams
- To develop belief in self and ability to achieve
- To identify goals to pursue (short term and long term)

Description of the activity

Ask the group members to think individually about some of the things they dream of accomplishing and some of the things that they want to have in the future. Have them jot a few of these down in their journals. Next, distribute magazines and have them work together as a group to decide which pictures to include on a "dream board" (see illustration) to represent some of each group member's dreams. Often the board will be filled with material possessions such as cars, houses, shoes, etc. After the group has completed the dream board ask them to turn it over and draw a line down the center. Ask them to write "Goals" at the top of one side and "Dreams" at the top of the other side. As a group, ask them to list the difference between goals and dreams on each side. A few examples include:

Dreams are things we want; goals are things we work to achieve.
Dreams seem to be far away; goals can be worked on over a period of time.
Dreams are big; goals can be broken down into steps.

Discuss as a group and explain why it is important to have both goals and dreams.

Variation of the activity

- Wants vs. Needs Board—Complete the above activity but use "Wants vs. Needs" instead of "Goals vs. Dreams."

DEAR YOUNGER SELF

Materials needed

- Paper

- Pencils

- Markers

Purpose of the activity

- To process some of the events of life

- To share wisdom and lessons learned with the group

- To understand the importance of mentoring

Description of the activity

Ask each group member to think back on some of the events of his or her life. Ask participants to think of something they wish they had known at the time or something they would do differently if given a chance to do things again. Ask them to write a letter to their younger self sharing this information (if desired, a drawing can be created to symbolize the lesson). Ask each group member to try to come up with a short statement to symbolize the whole incident (examples include "Be kind to others" or "Treat your family with respect"). After completing the activity ask group members to share their letter or drawing with the group. Discuss ways they can help others, and keep them from making some of the same mistakes they made.

Variations of the activity

- Words of Wisdom—Combine all of the summary statements from each person's story into a "Words of Wisdom" book. If desired, each person can write his or her statement on a piece of paper and decorate it. Make copies and create a book for each group member.

- Wisdom Wall—Hang a large piece of paper on the wall and invite group members to write their words of wisdom on the wall.

- Dear Younger Sibling—Ask group members to write a letter to a younger sibling or relative about some of the things they want him or her to accomplish and some of the mistakes they want him or her to avoid. Let group members choose what to do with their letters when complete (for example keep them in their journals or give them to their sibling).

REMOVING THE MASK

Materials needed

- Enough copies of the Mask Handout
- Card or poster-board
- Markers
- String
- Hole puncher

Purpose of the activity

- To understand the importance of "being yourself"
- To identify different "masks" we wear in public
- To understand ways to feel comfortable being "yourself"

Description of the activity

Discuss with the group the purpose of a mask (to hide or conceal self), reasons why people wear masks (fear, shame, embarrassment, etc.) and types of masks (defiance, over-achievement, addiction, etc.). Give each group member a Mask Handout to cut out and then trace on the card. Cut the mask out of the card and allow each group member to decorate it. When complete, punch holes and tie string through so that the mask can be worn. Ask group members to wear their masks for a while during group time. Discuss how they felt while wearing the mask (hidden? separate? lonely?) as well as healthy ways to "remove the mask" (confront fears, choose friends who allow you to be yourself, etc.).

Variation of the activity

- Mask Removal Party—At the end of the group, have a mask removal party. Hang the masks on the wall. Discuss the fact that while masks can be beautiful and pretty to look at, they keep us hidden and separate from others. We are more beautiful without our masks.

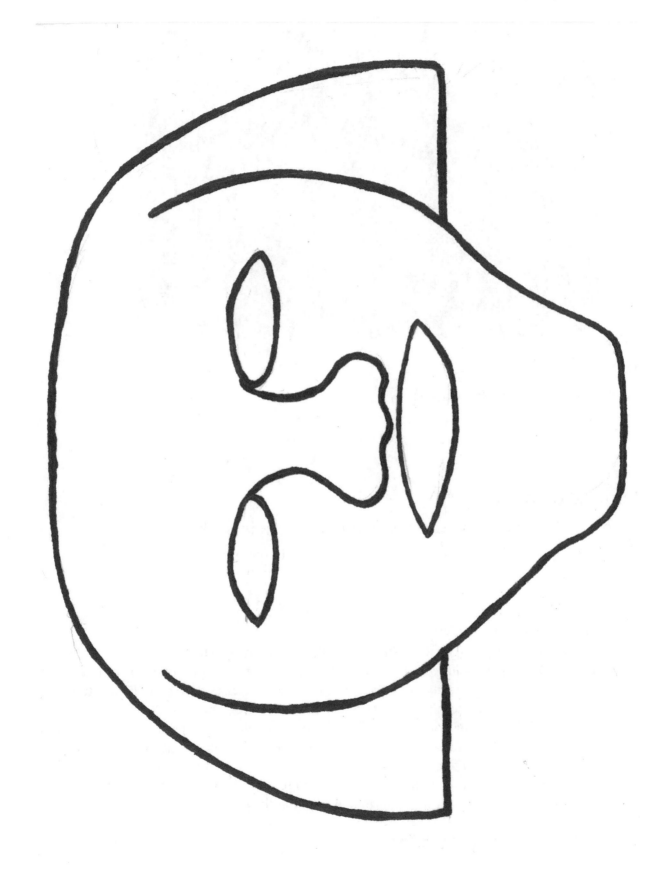

POSITIVE/NEGATIVE WORD WALLS

Materials needed

- Large paper (two pieces)
- Paint
- Tape

Purpose of the activity

- To identify the difference between positive and negative self-talk
- To learn ways to remove negative self-talk and expressions
- To encourage positive self-talk and expressions

Description of the activity

Start out by discussing some of the positive things we say to ourselves and others as well as some of the negative things. You will probably need to set some ground rules for this activity (such as no swearing or vulgarity). Some of the negative phrases that might be mentioned are "You're no good," "You can't do it," etc. Some of the positive phrases are "Great job," "I believe in you," etc. Spread out both large pieces of paper and let the groups create a Positive Word Wall (see illustration) and a Negative Word Wall. Discuss the words that were chosen for each wall as well as ways to focus on the positive, take what we can from the negative, and then let it go. Display the Positive Word Wall in the group room and let group members "destroy" the Negative Word Wall by tearing it up and putting it in the garbage.

SOUL SHINE SUNSHINE

Materials needed

- Yellow and orange card or construction paper
- Scissors
- Glue
- Markers
- CD player
- "Soulshine" song by the Allman Brothers Band (*Where it All Begins*, 1994)

Purpose of the activity

- To identify positive and healthy ways to express self
- To develop coping skills and problem-solving skills
- To encourage creativity, self-esteem, and self-expression

Description of the activity

This is a good activity for mature adolescents. Play the song for the group if possible. (Be aware that there is one minor swearword in the chorus of the song. Discuss with the adolescents ahead of time that the swearword is present in the song, but that the group will still listen to the song in order to discuss the message of the song lyrics. Ask them to be respectful by not acting silly or using the word in the group.) As a group, identify ways that a person could let his soul shine and ways to keep shining even in times of darkness and depression. Give each group member yellow and orange cardstock. Ask them to cut a large circle out of the yellow paper and use the remaining paper to trace their hands several times. Explain to them that they are going to create a "Soul Shine Sunshine." Ask them to use their hands as the rays and on each hand to write or draw a symbol for a way to let their soul shine. Share and discuss with the group when complete.

Variations of the activity

- "This Little Light of Mine"—This activity can also be used with younger children without the song or you can use another more appropriate song such as "This Little Light of Mine." Have them to identify ways to shine in the world.

- Handprint Creations—Many activities can be completed with handprints such as group flowers, wreaths, butterflies, etc. Let your imagination be your guide.

BEAD MEANING BRACELETS

Materials needed

- Round plastic beads (assorted colors and alphabet beads)
- String
- Scissors
- Index cards with explanations of meanings

Purpose of the activity

- To provide a visual reminder of therapeutic topics
- To develop coping skills
- To encourage problem-solving and anger control

Description of the activity

Most children love to bead and make jewelry. This activity can be used to help participants remember things that are discussed in the group. In addition to making the bracelet, have index cards with the meanings given below written on them for the group members to take (or have group members write the meanings themselves). Bracelets can be filled in using white, black, or clear beads. Some examples are:

Anger Control Bracelet
Red Bead = Stop and think
Blue Bead = Remain calm and don't overact
Yellow Bead = Proceed with caution
Green = Go and talk it out with a trusted friend

Believe in Me Bracelet
Blue Bead = I can do it
Green Bead = Keep on going for my goal
Red Bead = Don't let negativity stop me
Yellow = Have a good attitude

Word Bracelets
Spell out words such as CALM, PEACE, BELIEVE, or HOPE as a reminder of a particular therapeutic lesson. Fill in with colored beads as desired.

ZOO CREW/JUNGLE PEOPLE

Materials needed

- Large paper
- Paint
- Markers
- Tape

Purpose of the activity

- To promote group unity
- To develop social skills
- To encourage creativity and imagination

Description of the activity

Explain to the group that they are going to make a mural. Each group member will pick an animal to represent him or herself. As a group, they will decide whether to make a zoo mural or a jungle mural. All group members should contribute to the mural. When the mural is complete, discuss as a group the reasons for choosing zoo or jungle (this can often lead to interesting discussions about being comfortable but captive in the zoo, or free but at risk in the jungle). Also discuss each group member's animal choice and any interesting personality traits associated with each animal. Other interesting things to discuss include animal placement (who is close together, who is far apart), scenery, and background.

Variations of the activity

- Opposites Murals—Create murals using other choices for the group: City vs. Country, Sea vs. Land, Earth vs. Space…the possibilities are endless.
- Ideal Place Murals—Create a mural of an ideal school, amusement park, country… The possibilities are endless.

CREATIVE COOKBOOK

Materials needed

- Paper
- Recipes
- Markers
- Access to a printer or printing company
- Ingredients to test recipes

Purpose of the activity

- To encourage cooperation and social-skills development
- To promote healthy, functional living skills
- To encourage creativity and self-expression

Description of the activity

Begin by choosing a theme for the cookbook. One idea for a theme is "Cooking with Heart." Next, decide what sections to include. If using the heart theme, four sections are ideal:

- Heart Matters (group member's favorite family recipes)
- Recipes We Love (kid-friendly recipes)
- From Our Heart to Yours (staff favorites)
- Heart Healthy (nutritious recipes)

Ask the children to bring their favorite family recipe or a recipe that has a meaningful story to their family for the "Heart Matters" section. During group time, have the children create art or write a short essay about why the recipe is their favorite. Include these throughout the cookbook. Have a contest for the cover art, back cover art, and art for each of the section cover pages using the heart theme. For the "Recipes We Love" section, use recipes that are easy to make for kids. Ask staff to bring recipes for the "From Our Heart to Yours" section. For the "Heart Healthy" section, partner with a local dietician (if possible) and discuss nutrition as a group. Ask the dietician to provide you with some healthy recipes to include in the cookbook. Test as many of the recipes as possible with the group. When the activity is complete, make copies (however your budget allows) of the cookbook for each member of the group. Depending on your setting, be careful of confidentiality concerns about including names or identifying information in the cookbook.

Variations of the activity

- Giving from the Heart—If funding allows, donate copies of the cookbook to local dieticians, soup kitchens, or the chamber of commerce to be distributed.
- If your setting allows, sell copies of the cookbook to fund additional program supplies and materials to continue creative projects.

WHAT'S BUGGING ME?

Materials needed

- Enough copies of the Bug Handout
- Construction paper
- Pencils/markers
- Scissors
- Glue

Purpose of the activity

- To identify potential triggers for anger and annoyance
- To encourage healthy conflict-resolution skills
- To develop appropriate coping skills

Description of the activity

Discuss as a group and ask each individual to identify some things that "bug" them or get on their nerves. Distribute a Bug Handout and other needed materials to each student. Ask them to cut out the bug outline and trace onto the construction paper. Next, ask participants to cut the bug out of the construction paper. On each of the bug's legs, ask them to list one thing that bugs them. Once this is complete, discuss as a group ways to handle it when things bug us. Assist the participants in identifying at least one way to cope with each thing that bugs them. Ask them to flip over their bug and list one of their coping skills on each of the bug's legs. Share the final results with the group.

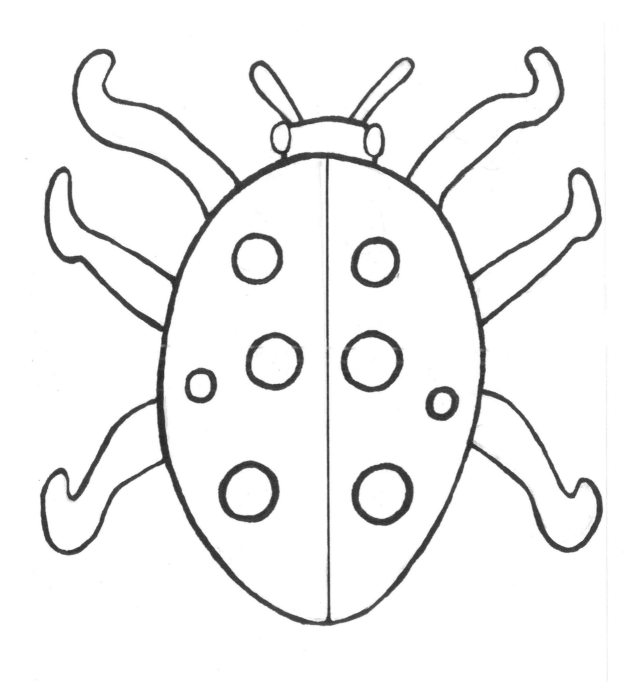

SOCIAL BUTTERFLIES

Materials needed

- Enough copies of the Butterfly Handout
- Construction paper
- Scissors
- Glue
- Pencils/markers

Purpose of the activity

- To identify appropriate social skills
- To discuss ways to develop or improve socials skills
- To develop self-esteem

Description of the activity

Discuss social skills with the group and assist the group in identifying appropriate social skills. Let each group member identify an area in which he or she thinks they need improvement with social skills. Distribute the Butterfly Handout and other needed supplies. Ask participants to cut out the butterflies and trace them onto the construction paper (or white paper/card if students would like to decorate the butterflies). Ask them to list some examples of good social skills on their butterflies. Let them decorate the other side of their butterfly. Discuss the responses as a group and display the butterflies in the group room.

Butterfly Handout

CHAPTER 4

Month-by-Month Character Education Calendar

The character education ideas and activities in this chapter relate closely to holidays and events in the United States calendar. Those in other countries may choose to take the ideas and/or activities and adapt them to their own country's holidays, traditions, and significant events. Many of the activities would work well at any time of the year and can easily be adapted.

January

CHINESE DRAGONS (NEW YEAR'S DAY)

Materials needed

- Card or construction paper
- Scissors
- Glue
- Enough copies of the Chinese Dragon Handout
- Pencils
- Information on the Chinese New Year

Purpose of the activity

- To express goals for the year
- To commit to working toward goals and identify steps to accomplish goals
- To develop self-expression and creativity

Description of the activity

Explain the tradition of the Chinese New Year Dragons to the group. The dragon is one of the symbols of the Chinese New Year; it symbolizes goodness, poise, strength, and supernatural power to the Chinese people. As part of the New Year festivities, a parade is held and the

Chinese people dress as dragons and dance down the streets. Discuss the tradition of setting goals and resolutions for the New Year. Ask each group member to identify some things he or she would like to change, work on, or improve over the next year. Discuss ways to break goals into smaller steps, to maintain motivation, and to stay on course. Give out the Chinese Dragon Handout, several pieces of construction paper (let participants choose several different colors), glue, scissors, and pencils. Ask group members to cut out the template and trace onto construction paper. Next, ask them to cut the dragon out of construction paper. They should also cut out strips to serve as the dragon's tail. On each of the tail strips, the participant will write one of his or her goals for the year. Each participant can use as many strips as needed. Share with the group and display when complete.

cut 3

"I HAVE A DREAM" DAY (DR. MARTIN LUTHER KING, JR.'S BIRTHDAY)

Materials needed

- Large paper
- Enough copies of the Star Handout
- Construction paper (all same color)
- Brief biography of Dr. Martin Luther King, Jr. (see the Resources list)

- Scissors
- Tape
- Markers
- Certificates

Purpose of the activity

- To encourage positive thinking and achievement
- To discuss positive ways to handle opposition
- To develop social skills and self-esteem

Description of the activity

This activity will help encourage children while at the same time educating them on Dr. Martin Luther King, Jr. and his impact on the USA. Begin by giving children an overview of Dr. King's life. A few points to touch on include:

- his nonviolent approach to conflict
- whether his dreams seemed possible at the time
- what motivated him
- how he brought people together.

Distribute copies of the Star Handout to participants. Explain to the children that there will be an "I Have a Dream" Day on the set date. Explain to them that they will be thinking about some of their dreams and will put their dreams on the stars to present at the "I Have a Dream" Day. If possible, get a large piece of paper (blue if possible) and have someone draw a picture of Dr. King in the middle and write in large letters "We Have Dreams" at the top. If your setting allows, have a ceremony to commemorate the "I Have a Dream" Day. Let each child come up and present his or her dreams to the group and then hang the stars listing the dreams on the large paper. Present each child with a certificate for participating in the program. If possible serve a special snack such as cake or ice-cream.

Star Handout

RECIPE FOR SUCCESS/"WHEN DREAMS COME TRUE" DAY (DR. MARTIN LUTHER KING, JR.'S BIRTHDAY)

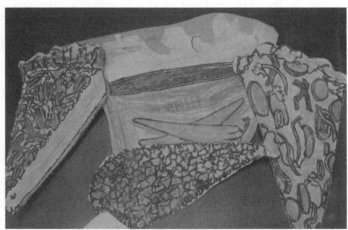

Materials needed

- Enough copies of the Recipe Card Handout (see p.58)

- Markers/pencils

- Scissors

- Large paper (two pieces)

- Enough copies of the food outline handouts

- Construction paper

- Trail mix materials

- Airtight plastic bags

- Printed copies of the trail mix's meaning

- Certificates for participation

Purpose of the activity

- To develop self-esteem and social skills

- To identify and understand ways to achieve goals

- To increase awareness of important historical figures

Description of the activity

There are several different activities for this lesson that will all end with a "When Dreams Come True" Day. We completed this series the year that President Obama was elected. The focus was on continuing to believe in yourself until dreams begin to come to true. Throughout the week in the group, several activities were completed leading up to the "When Dreams Come True" ceremony. All of the lessons are focused on food and creating a "Recipe for Success."

The first activity involved making a personal recipe for achieving personal goals. Each participant will need a copy of the Recipe Card Handout. Ask each person to identify a goal and break it down into a recipe (for example a tablespoon of patience, a cup of hard work, a spoonful of generosity). Combine all the recipes into a book.

The second activity involved creating a "Meaningful Trail Mix" that the group would make at the "When Dreams Come True" ceremony. Two examples of this are given below, but please encourage your groups to create their own.

The third activity involved learning about President Obama and Dr. Martin Luther King, Jr. (see short biographies below). Due to the food focus of these activities, we researched the favorite foods of both men, which included pizza and chili (President Obama) and fried chicken and pecan pie (Dr. Martin Luther King, Jr.). Print copies of the food outline handouts and allow children to select which food they want to use for their goal. Each child will cut out the template, trace it onto construction paper and cut it out. On the back of the food, he or she will write one of his or her goals or dreams and then color and decorate the front of the food. For the "When Dreams Come True" Day, have someone draw pictures of President Obama and Dr. Martin Luther King, Jr. onto the large paper. Give all participants the opportunity to present their dream and then attach it (based on which food was chosen) to the appropriate person. Give each child a certificate of participation for completing the event. For a snack, make one of the meaningful trail mixes (see below).

Information about Dr. Martin Luther King, Jr.'s life

Dr. Martin Luther King, Jr. was a key figure in the American Civil Rights movement. He changed the culture of the United States of America by fighting for the civil rights of African-Americans using a nonviolent approach. His birthday is celebrated as a national holiday each January in the United States. The values and story of his life are applicable not only to citizens of the United States, but to people all over the world. Dr. King is recognized as an important individual worldwide. For a detailed biography of his life, please visit www.thekingcenter.org/drmlkingjr.

Information about President Barack Obama

President Barack Obama is the 44th President of the United States of America. He is the first African-American president of the country. For a detailed biography of his life, visit www.whitehouse.gov/about/presidents/barackobama.

Variation of the activity

- Choose any living African-American with good character and a "successful" image to serve as the "When Dreams Come True" representative.

Be sure to remind children that while achieving dreams can sometimes happen in "one moment" (such as being elected president), there is a lot of hard *before* and *after* achieving our goals.

"When Dreams Come True" Trail Mix

CELEBRATING DR. MARTIN LUTHER KING, JR. AND PRESIDENT BARACK OBAMA

Sunflower Seeds—Represent planting seeds for our future

Small chocolate candies—Represent memories of Dr. King

Pretzels—Represent holding on to the dream of Dr. King

"Red Hots" spicy, cinnamon candy—Represent the love in our hearts

Chips—Represent not crumbling under pressure

Raisins—Represent the respectful people that we strive to be

"When Dreams Come True" Trail Mix

CELEBRATING DR. MARTIN LUTHER KING, JR. AND PRESIDENT BARACK OBAMA

Kisses or Lovehearts—Represent the love we have for each other

Chocolate candies with a peanut center—Represent the strong heart inside each individual

Raisins—Represent the will to change from a grape to a raisin in the sunshine

Small chocolate candie—Represent the many different colors and races of people mixing together to create the rainbow of life

Pretzels—Represent the ties that bind as we look into the future

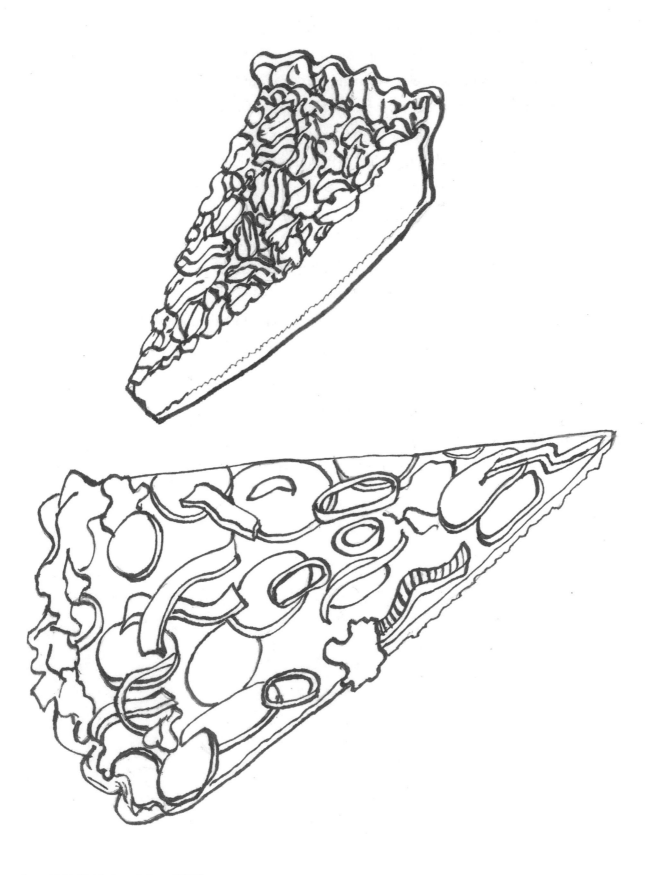

Chili and Fried Chicken Handout

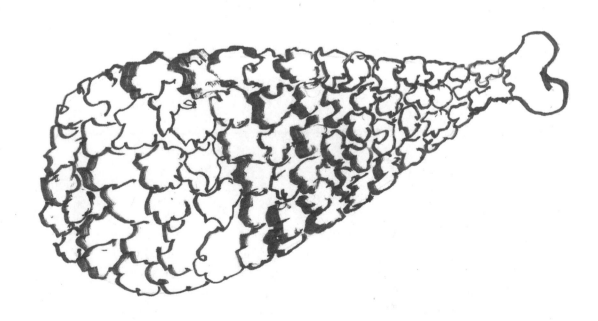

February

STUFFED WITH LOVE (VALENTINE'S DAY)

Materials needed

- Newspaper and scrap paper
- Paint
- Paint brushes
- Scissors
- Stapler

Purpose of the activity

- To develop social skills and self-esteem
- To discuss ways to show love to others
- To develop creativity

Description of the activity

For a Valentine's Day activity, discuss love and healthy ways to show love to parents, friends, and family members. Examples might be hugs, completing chores without being asked, sharing with a sibling, etc. Divide group members into pairs and assign each pair a work area. Lay out extra newspaper to protect the floor from paint. Cut large hearts (two per pair) out of the remaining newspaper. Let each pair paint their two hearts as desired. Let them dry. When the hearts are dry, begin stapling them together, but leave enough room for children to stuff the middle of the heart with extra newspaper or scrap paper (see illustration). When the hearts are full of paper, finish the stapling. Display in the room or allow each pair to decide on a teacher or other school employee to give their heart to as a Valentine's Day gift.

Variation of the activity

- Almost any shape desired can be made using this method. Examples include easter eggs, candy canes, and pumpkins.

CANDY CARDS (VALENTINE'S DAY)

Materials needed

- Assorted candy (see below for examples)
- Markers
- Poster-board
- Masking tape or glue

Purpose of the activity

- To show love and kindness to others
- To identify reasons and benefits of showing love to others
- To be creative

Description of the activity

This activity will allow the group to create unique and fun Valentine's Day cards using candy. Take the piece of poster-board and fold it in half. Choose some of the phrases below and write them on the poster-board leaving a spot to attach the candy using the masking tape. To create smaller cards, trim the poster-board to the size of a piece of paper and choose one candy phrase to include. Examples are listed below of various poems or phrases with which candy can be used. The name of the type of candy needed is in italics. Be creative: The ideas for using candy in phrases are endless. Many of the candies listed are mainly available in the United States. If you live in another country, you may adapt the phrases to suit the candies available in your country.

I'm *Red-Hot* [red cinnamon candies] for you!
You'll always be my *Milky Way* [candy bar] on earth because there will never be another *Starburst* [chewy fruit candy] in *Orbit* [chewing gum] like you.
You make me feel like *100 Grand* [candy bar] when you give me hugs and *Kisses* [chocolate candy].
I think about you *Now and Later* [chewy fruit candy].
You bring me *Joy* [Almond Joy candy bar].
If you need me, I will be there in a *New York* [chocolate mint candy] minute [an instant].

Variation of the activity

- Icebreaker/Closer—Use candy cards to get feedback from group members about the session or to start the group off. Examples are listed below; write these phrases on small pieces of paper or poster-board and attach the candy using masking tape. Distribute these to the members of the group either at the beginning of the group as an icebreaker, or the end of the group to get feedback. Ask group members to respond (this could be a verbal or written response according to the group leader's preference) to the question or phrase on the candy card.

- I know you don't want to be an *Airhead* or *Laffy Taffy* [chewy fruit candy], so please tell me a few things you would like to get out of this group.

- Please tell me something that brought you *Joy* [Almond Joy candy bar] in today's group.

- Please be a *Smartie* [fruit-flavored candy] and tell me something that could make the group better.

RHYTHM AND BLUES (BLACK HISTORY MONTH)

I merely took the energy it takes to pout and wrote some blues.

Duke Ellington

Materials needed

- CD of some Blues music
- Examples of Blues artwork for viewing (visit www.longriver.net/hunt.html for examples of Blues artwork by George Hunt)
- Paper
- Pencils
- Blue art supplies (construction paper, paint, glitter, markers, tissue paper, etc.)
- Brief history of Blues music (visit www.blues.org for blues history)

Purpose of the activity

- To identify ways to turn "negative" events into "positive" events
- To identify and utilize appropriate coping skills
- To develop social skills and teamwork

Description of the activity

Discuss the Blues with your group. Give them a brief overview of how Blues music began. Explain to them that many Blues musicians grew up in difficult circumstances but used music to turn their circumstances into something positive. Also, discuss "Blues" and the association with depression and feeling "blue." Ask group members to give an example of something in their life that started out being a "bad" thing but turned into a "good" thing. Distribute art supplies and ask group members to create a "blue" work of art. Share and discuss when complete.

Variations of the activity

- Singing the Blues—Pair group members up and ask each pair to write their own Blues song. Share with the group.
- Blues Trail—Provide group members with a US map outline (available at www.eduplace. com/ss/maps/pdf/us_nl.pdf; this map can be reproduced for personal and classroom use) and give them some events in Blues history to research (use an internet search engine) and then draw the journey on the United States map. This activity could also be incorporated into a Social Studies setting.

BLACK HISTORY PROGRAM (BLACK HISTORY MONTH)

Materials needed

- Poster-board (one for each group)
- Markers
- List of famous African-Americans
- CD player
- Props as needed

Purpose of the activity

- To identify positive character traits in famous African-Americans
- To promote acceptance and diversity
- To develop social skills and teamwork skills

Description of the activity

Discuss Black History Month (celebrated in February in the United States and Canada, and celebrated in October in the United Kingdom) and the importance of celebrating the men and women who made a difference to the lives of future generations. Tell the group that they are going to make a poster about a famous African-American. As part of their poster presentation, they may use music, props or make up a skit if desired. If you have several different groups, let each group choose a person and then let all the groups watch the other poster presentations. This could be incorporated into a Social Studies class. If desired, have a contest between the groups to increase motivation and participation.

Examples of famous Black people include:

Diane Abbott	Rosa Parks
Maya Angelou	Colin Powell
Bill Cosby	Condoleezza Rice
Morgan Freeman	Coretta Scott King
Lewis Hamilton	Tina Turner
Langston Hughes	Desmond Tutu
B.B. King	George Washington Carver
Nelson Mandela	Oprah Winfrey
Michelle Obama	

March

POT OF GOLD SCAVENGER HUNT (ST. PATRICK'S DAY)

Materials needed

- Colored envelopes (red, yellow, green, blue, purple)
- Clues to lead through the Scavenger Hunt
- Tape
- Prize for finding the Pot of Gold (ideas include a Group Pizza Party or Ice-Cream Party)

Purpose of the activity

- To develop following directions skills
- To improve teamwork skills
- To increase social skills and cooperation

Description of the activity

Begin this activity the week before St. Patrick's Day. Explain to the group that they are going to have a Pot of Gold Scavenger Hunt this week. Each day they will have a clue to find. Give them the first clue that day. Depending on your setting, you could just hide the clues each day in the group room or if you are in a school setting you could put the clue somewhere to be found while going to lunch. Make up the clues based on the age of your group and their ability level. Try to make up clues that will require the group members to work together and discuss ideas about where the next clue could be. If possible, make the clue a short poem or rhyme with information about the next clue. On the last day, let the clue lead the group to a Pot of Gold. This could be a pot full of candy and snacks for the group to enjoy, a coupon for a Group Pizza Party, or a coupon for a Group Ice-Cream Party. After the scavenger hunt is over, discuss with the group what they had to do to find and solve the clues (follow directions, work together, etc.).

Variation of the activity

- Complete in One Day—If the above activity will not work for you, consider taking a field trip to a local park. Hide the clues on the morning of the trip and let the group complete the entire scavenger hunt in one day. Let the final clue bring them back to an Ice-Cream Party in the park.

TAKE A (SPRING) BREAK AND RELAX (SPRING BREAK)

Materials needed

- CD player
- Mixed CD which includes several different types of music (see checklist)
- A range of different fragrance oils
- Copy of Relaxing music checklist for each person (see below)
- Copy of Aromatherapy checklist for each person (see below)

Purpose of the activity

- To learn healthy ways to relax
- To develop coping skills
- To identify personal ways to self-soothe and calm down

Description of the activity

Many children have difficulty relaxing and coping with stress. This is a fun way to help them identify some music and scents that will help them cope with stress and relax. Begin by giving each participant the "Relaxing music checklist." Ask participants to get comfortable in their seats. Tell them you are going to play some different types of music for them. Play a 30–45 second sample of each type of music and tell them what type of music it is if they do not know. Ask the group members to put a check mark (tick) by the types of music they find soothing. If resources allow, let each group member create a mixed CD of the types of music they personally have chosen.

After playing all the different types of music, discuss some of the different choices.

- Did everyone pick the same thing? Why, or why not?
- How can you use the music to relax and cope with stress?

For the aromatherapy activity, give all participants a copy of the "Aromatherapy checklist." Tell them you are going to ask them to smell some different scents and choose the ones that are relaxing and calming to them. Ask them to get comfortable in their seats. Announce the name of each scent and walk slowly around the room with the scent. Give each member five to ten seconds to smell each scent. Ask them to put a check mark beside the scents that were relaxing to them. If resources allow, let each group member take home a sample of the scent chosen. After the activity, discuss the role of our senses in our relaxation and stress management. How can we use our senses to calm down?

When completing the aromatherapy activity, the group leader should take precautions to protect the participants. Be sure not to put the oil too close to the child's nose. Instead, consider using a paper wand or cotton swab that can be smelled but held away from the nose. Remind the children that some of the oils have strong smells and they should only sniff the oil. Keep the oils in a location away from the participants to prevent spills. If a child has a strong reaction to any of the oils, seek medical attention as needed.

Variations of the activity

- Identify ways to use the other senses (touch, sight, taste) to relax and manage stress appropriately. Examples include massage, positive touches (such as hugs or pats on the back), watching a film or looking at a book with soothing images, and eating a healthy diet.

- Edit the checklists as desired. These are just a jumping-off point for ideas.

Relaxing music checklist

☐ Jazz   ☐ Gospel

☐ Soft Rock   ☐ Classical

☐ Blues   ☐ Big Band music

☐ Hard Rock   ☐ R&B

☐ Rap   ☐ Instrumental

Aromatherapy checklist

☐ Lavender   ☐ Apple

☐ Mint   ☐ Hyacinth

☐ Lemon   ☐ Gardenia

☐ Peppermint   ☐ Pine

April

APRIL SHOWERS BRING MAY FLOWERS

Materials needed

- White or light-colored umbrellas
- Acrylic paint
- Paint brushes
- Bowls to hold paint

Purpose of the activity

- To identify ways to cope with stressful times
- To develop positive thinking and perspective
- To encourage creativity and self-expression

Description of the activity

Umbrellas protect us from bad weather, but we have to be willing to open our umbrellas and use them. Discuss how umbrellas can relate to ways to deal with stress and "storms" in our lives. Let the participants identify healthy coping skills and ways to use them in their own stressful situations. Give each participant an umbrella and painting supplies. Let them create their own umbrella of protection to serve as a reminder to use healthy coping skills when faced with stressful situations. Let each group member decorate his or her umbrella as desired (see illustration). Discuss the completed umbrellas and the meaning of the artwork on the umbrellas.

PEACEFUL EARTH (EARTH DAY)

Materials needed

- Foam-board
- Markers
- Paint (if desired)
- Pencils

- Old magazines
- Glue
- Scissors

Purpose of the activity

- To develop social skills and self-esteem
- To increase nature appreciation
- To promote empathy

Description of the activity

Before the group begins, draw a large picture of the earth on the foam-board. When the group arrives, explain that today is Earth Day. Discuss the importance of caring for the earth as well as the people and animals that live on earth. Let the group identify ways to take care of earth and show we care for others. Give the group the foam-board with earth drawn on it and ask them to create a "Peaceful Earth" using symbols, images or words. After the project is complete, discuss the symbols chosen by the group and why these were chosen. Display the project in the group room.

Variations of the activity

- Earth Response—Ask group members to write a short response in their journals about the earth's reaction (how the child thinks the earth would feel about the images and symbols that they have created—happy, sad, relieved, etc.) to their images and symbols. Share and discuss.

- Nature Walk—Go on a nature walk and collect materials such as rocks and leaves to include on the "Peaceful Earth" project.

May

GROWING A GARDEN OF MENTAL HEALTH (CHILDREN'S MENTAL HEALTH WEEK)

Growing a Garden of Mental Health

Materials needed

- Enough copies of the Flower Handout
- Construction paper
- Large piece of paper
- Scissors
- Tape
- Markers

Purpose of the activity

- To identify ways to promote mental health and wellness
- To emphasize healthy coping skills
- To develop social skills and self-esteem

Description of the activity

Before beginning the activity, draw several large flower pots or a garden background on the large paper. Explain to the group that this week is National Children's Mental Health Week (held during May in the United States) and, as a group, identify some ways to stay mentally healthy (getting enough sleep, taking time for yourself, exercising, etc.) Tell the group that they are going to create a Garden of Mental Health. Give each group member a copy of the Flower Handout and have him or her cut it out, glue it on to construction paper, and cut it out to make it sturdy. On each of the flower petals, ask the group members to identify ways they can stay mentally healthy. After this is complete, let each group member decorate his or her flower as desired. When all are complete, discuss as a group and add to the garden (see illustration).

Flower Handout

STEP BY STEP (GARDENING ACTIVITIES)

Materials needed

- Assorted garden tools
- Potting soil
- Pots
- Garden soil
- Plants
- 12 x 12 inch (30 x 30 centimeter) concrete stepping stones
- Bricks
- Acrylic paint
- Sealer for stepping stones
- Small colorful stones
- Cups
- Yarn
- Fabric glue

Purpose of the activity

- To develop responsibility
- To encourage social skills and self-esteem
- To promote empathy

Description of the activity

This activity can be as simple or complex as you desire. If you have the space at your facility, plant a small garden. If possible, consult an experienced gardener for advice and help. Before involving the group, have the ground tilled and ready to be planted. If you have some older children in your group, let them dig the holes and plant the plants. Assign tasks to each group member to help with the maintenance of the garden (watering, weeding, fertilizing, etc.). Be sure to rotate tasks so that each group member has an opportunity to complete each task. Watch the garden grow and enjoy as a group.

Variations of the activity

- Gardening Journal—Once a week, have group members journal about the garden, the new plants growing and blooming, and their feelings about the garden. This will become a written history of the garden.

- Group Stepping Stone—Let the group work together and create an artistic stepping stone to become part of the garden. The stones should represent the whole group. Use acrylic paint and then seal when dry to preserve. If desired, add stones (attached with fabric glue) to give more interest to the stones.

- Individual Stepping Stones—Give each group member a brick and allow him or her to decorate it to reflect his or her personality using acrylic paint and stones (see illustration). Let dry, seal, and add to the group garden.

- Class Plant—If space is not available for a garden at your facility, then consider having a class plant. Let the group paint the flower pot and choose what kind of plant to grow. As with the garden, assign jobs to group members to care for the plant.

- Mother's Day Gift—Give all the children a plastic cup and, using fabric glue, show them how to slowly and carefully wrap the yarn around the cup. The entire cup will end up being covered by yarn. Cut the yarn when complete and poke a tiny hole in the bottom of the cup. Fill with potting soil and flower of choice (begonias work well). Let the group members take them to their mother or another special person on Mother's Day.

June

BEAD BUDDIES

Materials needed

- Pipe cleaners (assorted colors)
- Wooden beads (assorted colors)
- Scissors

Purpose of the activity

- To encourage generosity
- To develop healthy social skills
- To encourage self-esteem

Description of the activity

Ask the children to identify their best friend. Discuss friendship and ways to treat others. Give each child six pipe cleaners and ten assorted wooden beads. Explain to the children that they are going to create a bead buddy to represent themselves and their best friend. Show the children how to twist two pipe cleaners together to make an "X." This will be the person's arms and legs. Have them cut another one of the pipe cleaners in half and wrap it one time around the center of the "X." This will be the person's upper body and head. Now have each child add a bead to the end of each arm, leg, and the head. Twist pipe cleaners to secure beads onto the person. Now repeat the process to make the bead buddy to represent their best friend. When complete, let children give the bead buddy to their friend as a "friendship" gift.

ANGER-CONTROL TOTEM POLES

Materials needed

- Wooden dowels (about 5 feet/1.5 meters tall) or yard/meter sticks will work for small groups
- Masking tape
- Card
- Markers
- Scissors
- Enough copies of the animal templates
- Enough copies of the Animal Anger-Control Questionnaire

Purpose of the activity

- To identify anger-control styles
- To learn ways to manage anger in an appropriate way
- To gain self-knowledge and insight

Description of the activity

Give participants an Animal Anger-Control Questionnaire and ask them to answer the questions in order to identify their "anger animal." Discuss the different anger animals and how they tend to respond when angry. As a group discuss appropriate anger-management skills (such as deep breathing, taking time to cool down, journaling, listening to music, etc.) and ways to develop these skills. Distribute the animal handouts and other supplies. Have the group members trace their chosen anger animal onto the card and cut it out. Let them decorate these as desired. When complete, use masking tape to tape each animal to the wooden dowel and create an anger-control totem pole (see illustration).

Animal Anger-Control Questionnaire

Please circle the item that most describes you when you are angry.

1. Which one do you look the most like when you are angry?

    A. Teddy bear (No one would know I am mad)

    B. Dog (I complain and fuss but don't do anything about it)

    C. Lion (I get mad and hit, fight, or act aggressively toward others)

    D. Cat (I lash out and pout when I am angry)

    E. Rabbit (I get really upset/hyper and have trouble calming down)

    F. Pig (I get upset and want to eat)

    G. Donkey (I tend to act before I think when I am mad)

    H. Elephant (I never forget why I am angry and hold onto it forever)

2. When I am angry, I often…

    A. wish someone would notice.

    B. complain so everyone knows I am mad.

    C. take it out on someone (whoever is in my way).

    D. pout and stay mad for a long time.

    E. get really upset and can't be still.

    F. eat, eat, eat. Chocolate, anyone?

    G. act without thinking and then wish I hadn't.

    H. remind the person of what they did all the time.

3. You can tell I'm angry if…

    A. you wouldn't know.

    B. I am fussing about the same thing for a long time.

    C. I am yelling at or otherwise harassing someone.

    D. I am pouting and giving you one-word answers to every question.

    E. I am walking around in circles and have been for hours.

    F. the refrigerator is empty.

    G. someone is crying and I am regretting what I impulsively did.

    H. I am talking about something that made me mad five years ago.

SCORING

Mostly As—Teddy bear (Stuffs feelings)

Mostly Bs—Dog (All bark and no bite)

Mostly Cs—Lion (All bite)

Mostly Ds—Cat (Hisses and holds grudges)

Mostly Es—Rabbit (Hops around and won't calm down)

Mostly Fs—Pig (Emotional eater)

Mostly Gs—Donkey (Acts foolishly without thinking)

Mostly Hs—Elephant (Never forgets)

HEALTHY WAYS TO HANDLE ANGER

1. Take several deep breaths and relax before acting.

2. Count yourself down until you are feeling calm.

3. Think of a happy memory or place.

4. Give yourself some space to calm down and decide how to handle the situation.

5. It is okay to be angry but it's not okay to say or do things to hurt others.

6. After you have time to cool off, talk about your feelings to a safe person.

Teddy Bear Handout

119

Dog Handout

Lion Handout

121

Rabbit Handout

123

Pig Handout

Donkey Handout

125

July

GROUP SAND CASTLES

Materials needed

- Play sand (available at home improvement stores)
- Inflatable pools (approximately 3 feet/1 meter in diameter)
- Sand molds
- Access to a water hose

Purpose of the activity

- To expose participants to new activities
- To develop social skills
- To encourage leisure activities and creativity

Description of the activity

Many of the children I work with have never been outside of the small town we live in. This activity is a great way to expose them to something they might not otherwise experience. Before the children arrive, blow up the inflatable pools in an outdoor location. Add a small amount of water to the bottom of the pool (enough to make the sand pliable) and put the play sand in the pool. Set the sand molds around. Create as many stations as needed, but about four children per sand castle works well. When children arrive, divide them into groups and let them have fun creating the sand castles. Observe the interactions between the group members as they are working on their castles. When the activity is complete, let each group present their sand castle to the other groups. Discuss any issues related to working in the group.

SAND ART

Materials needed

- Plastic shapes to hold sand
- Several different colors of sand (see Resources section)
- Funnels
- Cups to hold the colored sand
- Tops to seal plastic shapes

Purpose of the activity

- To discuss relaxation and coping skills
- To develop social skills and self-esteem
- To encourage creativity

Description of the activity

As a group, talk about coping skills and ways to relax. Discuss places and things that can help us relax (the beach, clean sheets, being outdoors, etc.). Explain that many people are soothed by the beach, ocean waves, and sand. Tell them that today they are going to create some sand art to remind them to slow down and relax. Let each child pick his or her desired plastic shape (I have used butterflies, flowers, etc.) and then using the funnels let each child pour some of each of the different colored sands into his or her plastic shape. Remind the children not to shake the plastic shapes as the colors will "blend" together instead of staying separate. When complete, review coping skills and relaxation techniques. Ask the children to use this sand art as a reminder to relax during stressful times.

August

BACK TO SCHOOL SURVIVAL KIT

Materials needed

- Airtight plastic bags (quart size/ 1 liter)
- Enough copies of the Back to School Survival Kit Handout
- Pencil with an eraser on the end
- Rubber bands

- Sticky notes
- Small ruler
- Highlighter
- Crayons
- Safety scissors
- Paperclips

Purpose of the activity

- To encourage a positive attitude about going back to school
- To provide a visual reminder of important therapeutic concepts
- To develop self-esteem

Description of the activity

Discuss each group member's feelings about going back to school. Common feelings can include excitement, fear, sadness, and anxiety. Explain to the group that they are going to create a personal survival kit with basic school supplies to serve as a reminder of some important things discussed while participating in the group (although this activity also works well in an individual setting). Distribute the materials and a copy of the Back to School Survival Kit Handout to each person. (Each group member needs one of each of the items on the handout.) Review the meaning of each item together as a group and remind the group members that any time they feel nervous or afraid, they can look in their survival kit and see what tool they need to pull out.

Back to School Survival Kit Handout

Pencil with eraser—Remember to stay sharp, but if you make a mistake, admit it, apologize, and move on.

Rubber bands—Remember things don't always go as planned. Be flexible and make the best of negative situations.

Sticky notes—Remember it won't always be easy, but stick with it. It will be worth it in the end!

Small ruler—Remember to stay straight and follow the rules.

Highlighter—Remember to focus on the positive things in life.

Crayons—Remember to be creative and never lose the joy of learning something new.

Safety scissors—Remember to cut negative influences out of your life and stay safe and drug-free.

Paperclips—Remember we are all different in the way we look and the talents we have, but we all serve a valuable purpose.

SCHOOL PRIDE GUIDE

Materials needed

- Colored card
- White paper
- Markers
- Pens

- Scissors
- Information about your school (history, mascot, clubs, etc.)
- Photos of school

Purpose of the activity

- To promote school unity
- To welcome new students to the school
- To develop social skills

Description of the activity

This activity is a great way to build school pride and to welcome new students to school. This project can often be incorporated in Social Studies classes, with each class completing a different section. Suggestions for different sections include:

- A front covering featuring a drawing of the school or school mascot. You could make it into a contest between students if desired. It could also be incorporated into Art classes.
- School map.
- School history.
- School staff.
- Basic school information (address, phone, website).
- School mascot.
- Academics (curriculum, academic achievements, etc.).
- Clubs and activities.
- Athletics.
- School calendar.
- School publications (yearbook, newspaper).
- Special school features or achievements.

Assign each class a section or two to complete. Encourage them to research their section and be as creative as possible. Give them a page limit (usually one or two pages per section) and ask them to include important information and pictures about their topic. When all the sections are complete, combine and number the pages, and create a table of contents. If desired, include student artwork as the cover page for each section. When complete, duplicate and keep in the office to distribute as a welcome gift to new students.

September

TAILGATE PARTY

Materials needed

- Large paper
- Permanent black markers
- Football collector's cards (cut in half and separated)
- Umpire uniform (for an adult to wear)
- Plastic spoons
- Miniature football (one which fits onto a spoon)
- Grilling materials (hot dogs, buns, charcoal, etc.)

Purpose of the activity

- To promote good behavior and get children excited about school
- To develop social skills
- To encourage the following of directions

Description of the activity

This is a fun way to start the school year. Tailgate parties are often held in the fall (autumn) in the United States as an opportunity to socialize before and after football games. Tailgate parties are traditionally held with a variety of picnic foods (hamburgers, hot dogs, potato chips, dips, etc.) set up on the tailgate of a truck bed. The tailgate party typically begins before the football game and resumes after the game is over. If you live in an area where football and tailgating is not a popular activity, consider making the activities below applicable to another sport such as soccer. A suggestion for a theme that will work for a variety of sports is "Kicking off the Year with Good Behavior." The party can be set up with several stations that teach different character education themes such as following directions and social skills. If possible, grill hot dogs or have some other kind of special treat available. Listed below are some ideas for stations at the tailgate party.

- *Football Card Match-up*: Before the party, cut football cards apart and separate into sets of 20 each. There will need to be 20 children to participate each time this game is completed. Have half the children draw a card from one set and the other half of the children draw a card from the other set. Once everyone has drawn a card, tell the children to find their partner. Have a small prize for the first group to find their mate.

- *Umpire Says*: This game is just like the traditional game "Simon Says," but uses football moves as the instructions. If possible, get an adult to dress up as an umpire to lead the game. Have small prizes available at the station for the last few children in the game.

- *Football Relay*: Divide the participants into two equal-sized groups. Give each group a plastic spoon with a miniature football on it. Set a designated mark for the person to run to and then run back to the next member of their relay team. Participants can only use one hand to hold the spoon (they shouldn't hold the football in the spoon with their other hand). The first team to complete the relay wins.

- *Sign-in Wall*: Have a large piece of paper available with "Kicking off the Year with Good Behavior Tailgate Party" painted on it. Let the children sign their names and commit to good behavior. Display in a prominent place in your school after the event.

- *Pep Rally*: If possible, arrange for the high-school cheerleaders to come and put on a short pep rally for the students. Talk to the teachers at the high school and find out about some of the cheerleaders and football players who exhibit good character traits. Ask if these students can speak briefly to the children about the importance of good character.

FAMILY TREE (GRANDPARENTS' DAY)

Materials needed

- Enough copies of the Family Tree Handout
- Markers
- 8 x 10 inch (20 x 25 centimeter) picture mat (a pre-cut card picture frame)
- 8 x 10 inch (20 x 25 centimeter) frame (if possible)
- Shrink wrap or some kind of clear plastic covering

Purpose of the activity

- To show love and appreciation to grandparents
- To learn about family history and origins
- To identify different types of families

Description of the activity

Children today come from a wide variety of family situations. Many children live with grandparents or have grandparents as their primary caregivers. This activity makes a great gift for children to take to their grandparents on National Grandparents' Day (celebrated the first Sunday after Labor Day (which is the first Monday in September) in the United States). Before beginning the activity, send a letter home to parents (or guardians) asking for a brief family history to use in creating the family tree. Be mindful when completing this project of children who may be in foster care or other similar situations and adapt the project to meet their needs. Using the brief family history, have the children create a family tree on the handout and write a letter to their grandparents telling them what they love about them and their family. When these are complete, laminate and mat using 8 x 10 picture mats. If possible, provide frames or make a frame. If this is not possible then shrink-wrap so that the recipient can frame it. Let children take their family trees to their grandparents as a gift on Grandparents' Day.

Variation of the activity

- Grandparents' Day Ceremony—Consider inviting grandparents and having a special ceremony where children can talk about their families and present their family trees to their grandparents. Invite grandparents to stay for lunch or serve dessert in the classroom when the ceremony is over.

Family Tree Handout

October

SAFETY SPIDERS (HALLOWEEN)

Materials needed

- Enough copies of the Spider Handout
- Markers
- Scissors
- Glue

Purpose of the activity

- To develop functional living skills
- To identify ways to stay safe when out at night
- To encourage social skills

Description of the activity

Many children go "Trick or Treating" during the month of October and it is useful to help children identify some ways to stay safe during this event. Some examples include staying with a group of people, wearing reflective clothing, letting an adult check candy before eating it, and staying in well-lit neighborhoods. Once the group has identified several ways to stay safe while "Trick or Treating," give out the Spider Handout. Ask the children to cut out the spider and write one of the ways to stay safe on each of the spider's legs. On the spider's stomach, write the words "Safety Spider." Let the children color and decorate their spider when complete.

Spider Handout

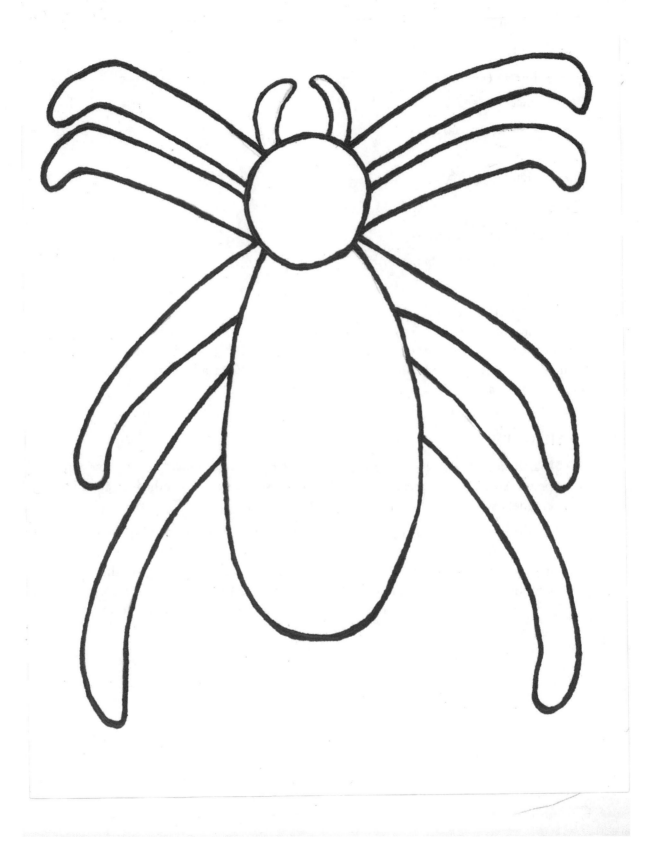

PAINTED PUMPKINS (HALLOWEEN)

Materials needed

- Small pumpkin
- Paint markers
- Glitter markers
- Table coverings
- Food for a special snack

Purpose of the activity

- To encourage creativity and self-expression
- To develop social skills
- To reward positive behavior

Description of the activity

This is a fun activity to use as special reward for good behavior or accomplishing a goal. Cover the work surface with paper or plastic so that paint does not get on it. Give each child a small pumpkin to paint and decorate as he or she chooses. When all the pumpkins are finished, display as a "Pumpkin Patch of Good Behavior."

Special snack ideas

- Marshmallow Spiders—Give each child a large marshmallow (for the spider's body), pretzel sticks (spider's legs), and small candies (spider's eyes). Let them create spiders and eat them.

- Koolaid Pickles (this may sound horrible, but they are really good!)—You will need a large 46 ounce (1.3 kilogram) jar of pickles and your desired flavor of Koolaid (fruit juice powder) mix prepared according to the directions. Pour out half of the pickle brine. Cut the pickles in half and put them back in the jar. Add the prepared Koolaid to the jar containing the pickles and the remaining pickle brine. Cover and refrigerate for at least 24 hours.

SCARING AWAY BAD BEHAVIOR (HALLOWEEN)

Materials needed

- Enough copies of the Mask Handout (see p.79)
- Card or poster-board
- Markers
- Glitter, sequins, and other trimmings to decorate the masks
- Glue

Purpose of the activity

- To identify reasons for inappropriate behavior
- To identify alternative ways of responding to upsetting situations
- To understand ways we may "hide" behind bad behavior

Description of the activity

Begin by discussing behavior with the group. Do most people act badly just to be mean? If not, why do they act this way? Assist the group in identifying some reasons for inappropriate behavior (hurt feelings, feeling lonely, not wanting others to see a perceived weakness, feeling hungry, tired, or frustrated with a difficult task, etc.). Ask each group member to think of an example of a time he or she acted inappropriately due to one of the identified reasons. Explain to the group that when we choose to act badly instead of addressing the real reason we are upset, it is like putting on a mask and hiding ourselves from others.

Give each group member a mask to color and decorate. As the group members are decorating their masks, discuss healthy ways to address some of the reasons for bad behavior (for example ask for a break, say how you feel, talk to a trusted adult, ask for help, etc.). Ask all group members to keep their masks as a visual reminder to be their "real" selves and to scare away the tendency to behave badly.

November

THANKFUL TURKEY (THANKSGIVING DAY)

Materials needed

- Large piece of paper with a turkey drawn on it
- Markers
- Scissors
- Tape
- Construction paper
- Enough card to make Thankfulness Certificates

Purpose of the activity

- To develop positive thinking and identify good things in life
- To promote coping skills
- To encourage self-esteem

Description of the activity

Thanksgiving is a holiday celebrated in the United States (on the fourth Thursday in November) and Canada (on the second Monday in October). Thanksgiving Day has its origins in a feast originally celebrated between pilgrims to America from England and Native Americans in 1621. Although the holiday has American roots, the theme of showing gratitude, thankfulness, and appreciation for the good things in life is applicable to people all over the world. Gratitude promotes positive thinking, and encourages hope and optimism in children.

At the beginning of the activity, provide children with a brief explanation of the Thanksgiving holiday and the importance of having gratitude for the good things in life. Ask the children to trace their hands and cut them out. On each finger, ask the children to list one thing in their life for which they are thankful. These hands will be the feathers for the turkey. After all the thankful hands are complete, have a Thankfulness Ceremony. Allow each child to come forward and tell the group about the things for which he or she is thankful. Next, help the child attach his or her hand to the back of the turkey as a feather. Give each child a certificate recognizing his or her participation in the Thankfulness Ceremony.

Special snack idea

- *Charlie Brown Thanksgiving Dinner*: After the Thankfulness Ceremony, host a Thanksgiving Dinner in the style of Charlie Brown (he served buttered toast and popcorn for his friends). Set up tables and chairs. Serve popcorn and toast with jelly. Watch *The Charlie Brown Thanksgiving Special* if possible. Encourage children to exhibit good table manners and social skills during the dinner.

✓

CERTIFICATE OF PARTICIPATION

THIS CERTIFICATE RECOGNIZES

. . . .

(NAME)

FOR THOUGHTFUL PARTICIPATION IN THE
THANKFULNESS CEREMONY ON

. . . .

(DATE)

THANK YOU FOR TAKING PART IN THIS SPECIAL DAY!

PRESENTED BY . . . .

DATE. . . . .

GIVING BACK BASKETS (THANKSGIVING DAY)

Materials needed

- Small baskets
- Brown, orange, or white gloves
- Orange, yellow, or brown felt
- Glue gun
- Cotton balls or filling to stuff gloves
- Markers
- Construction paper
- Leaves
- Ribbon
- Tissue paper
- Hard candies

Purpose of the activity

- To develop empathy for others
- To practice giving to others
- To learn social skills/cooperation in completing a group project

Description of the activity

Explain to the children that the group is going to create "Giving Back" Baskets to take to residents at local nursing home. Discuss some of the challenges that face nursing-home residents (loneliness, depression, bad health, etc.). Explain that nursing-home residents often don't have many visitors and many of the residents spend Thanksgiving at the nursing home.

Divide the group into three smaller groups. Assign one group (with the help of an adult) to stuff the gloves and glue them shut. Help them cut the felt to make a turkey beak and feathers to glue onto the glove. Assign a second group to use the construction paper and markers to create a card or poem to go in the basket. Ideas include using the letters in the word "Thanksgiving" to create a card, or finding inspirational quotes to add. Assign the third group to decorate the basket using the leaves, ribbon, tissue paper, and candy. When the baskets are complete, arrange for the group to deliver the basket to the nursing home and to go and meet some of the residents if possible.

December

WARM HANDS, WARM HEARTS

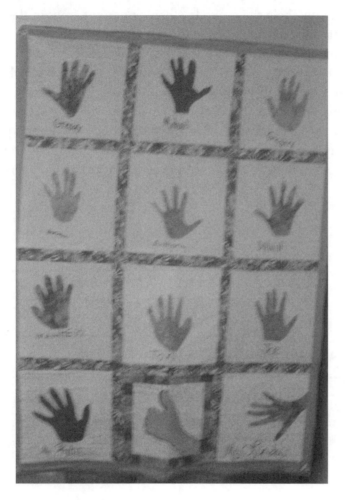

Materials needed

- Muslin or other fabric for the background of the quilt
- Assorted brightly colored fabrics for hands, back of quilt, and trim
- Fabric scissors
- Quilting needles
- Masking tape
- Batting (quilt filler)
- Iron-on adhesive
- Fabric marker

Purpose of the activity

- To develop patience and persistence
- To create a piece of art to reflect all group members
- To expose group members to new activities

Description of the activity

This is an involved project, but well worth the extra effort. If there is not a staff member with sewing or quilting knowledge, you may want to consider working with a seamstress or someone in your community who has knowledge of quilting in order to complete the project. Begin by letting each child choose one of the fabrics. Assist the child in tracing his or her hand onto the fabric and then cutting the handprint out.

Once all of the handprints are cut out, help the group lay them out on the front of the quilt (completed ahead of time and separated into a number of sections equal to the number of group members/handprints). After placing the handprints, allow each group member to write his or her first name or initials under his or her handprint. If possible, allow each group member to complete the preliminary sewing to stitch his or her handprint to the quilt. Next, complete the quilt by permanently attaching handprints, adding batting, and attaching the back of quilt (see illustration). Consider including the group name or an inspirational quote in one of the squares as well as handprints from the group leaders. When complete, display the quilt in a prominent place in the group room, or consider donating to a sick relative of one of the group members.

Quilt layout

Handprint	Handprint	Handprint
Handprint	Handprint	Handprint
Handprint	Group name/ Inspirational quote	Handprint
Handprint	Handprint	Handprint
Handprint	Handprint	Handprint

POLAR EXPRESS

Materials needed

- DVD of *The Polar Express* movie (Warner Brothers, 2004)
- Card
- Enough copies of the movie ticket to *The Polar Express* (see Movie Ticket Handout)
- Single hole punchers
- Medium-sized jingle bells (silver)
- Red ribbons

Purpose of the activity

- To develop positive-thinking skills/belief in self
- To identify some of the nonmaterial gifts in life
- To identify the joys of the Christmas season from a childlike perspective

Description of the activity

These are two meaningful activities to coordinate with the book or movie, *The Polar Express*. Ahead of time, copy the movie ticket onto the card. Discuss positive thinking with the group and reasons to believe in their self-worth and abilities. Explain that the group will be watching *The Polar Express* at the end of the week, but in order to be admitted, each group member must punch a positive word that describes him- or herself onto the movie ticket using the hole puncher. Examples of words include "smart," "fun," "pretty," "talented," etc.

During the week, while the group members work on punching their words, discuss the types of gifts people give and receive at Christmas. Assist the group members in identifying important nonmaterial gifts such as love, kindness, hope, and others. After watching the movie as a group, give each member a silver jingle bell with a red ribbon. Group members can use these as Christmas ornaments. Explain to the group that the jingle bell serves as a visual reminder of the lessons discussed in group during the week.

Special snack idea—Snowmen cakes

Ingredients needed:

- White cake mix (prepared according to directions as two round cakes (8 inches/20 centimeters)
- White icing
- Twizzler or similar rope-like chewy candy
- Jelly beans
- Small chocolate candies

Each snowman will feed approximately eight group members. After preparing the cakes, cover with white icing when the cakes have cooled. Use the chocolate candies as eyes, the Twizzler as the mouth, and jelly beans as the nose and buttons on the snowman. Enjoy!

✓

The Polar Express
MOVIE TICKET

ADMIT ONE

SHOWING ON . . . .

CHAPTER 5

Therapeutic Day Camp Activities and Day Program Ideas

Therapeutic day camps are a relatively new type of program for working with children and teens with behavioral and emotional problems. These camps provide the opportunity to teach a therapeutic skill in a fun, exciting environment utilizing hands-on activities and games. This approach creates teachable moments without making children feel like they are in a "therapy" session. Although the camps were originally developed for children and teens with emotional and behavioral problems, all children and teens could benefit from participating in the activities outlined in this chapter. The activities and concepts described could easily be adapted to other settings such as schools, churches, after-school programs, and childcare settings.

The activities described in this section can be conducted as a series of day camps, a single day camp, or as part of a field day or other school event. At the end of the chapter, a section is included with ideas for adapting the camps to different settings and group schedules. Typically, the day camps would last for five to six hours and be conducted weekly or bi-weekly for one to two months. The activities teach therapeutic lessons and skills using active games, art-therapy activities, and play-therapy approaches. In order to conduct the day camps, you will need a sufficient number of staff members or volunteers to supervise and assist with the activities, and a large open space to complete the activities. We typically held the camps in an outdoor setting with an open field, pavilions, and picnic tables, but the activities are adaptable to many settings (such as a school gym or meeting room with tables). Several staff members may be designated to serve as goal leaders and lead the goal progress check-in stations at each camp. (Information for the goal leaders is available on p.177.)

There are a few specific things that you can do to help the camps run smoothly:

- Plan ahead and arrive early to set up. Set up each station with all of the needed supplies before the participants arrive. A sample itinerary and supply list are included with each camp description to assist you in organizing and planning for the camps.

- Assign one or two staff members per ten children and allow these staff members to serve as the group leader or camp counselor for these participants at each camp. The group leader would lead the participants to each activity and assist them in completing the activity. This allows the participants to build a meaningful relationship with the group leader and the other participants in his or her group.

- Consider assigning specific staff members (who are not group leaders) to lead each station or activity in order to encourage continuity and allow the staff member to plan in advance for each station.

- Try to include one active station (with a game and movement) for every two more serious stations (stations that require sitting, reflecting, and listening).

- Many of the camps include a suggested afternoon reward based on behavior and participation at the camp. This will encourage and motivate the participants to exhibit good behavior and participate in the camp activities.

- If you conduct the camps as a series, the final camp can include a ceremony and reward day. Based on your community, the size of your group, and your budget, your reward activities may vary. Some of the rewards I have used included: swimming at the local community pool, going to the movies (be sure it is age- and theme-appropriate for your audience), playing at the playground, bowling, skating, and spending the day at the local waterpark.

- If desired, you can use a pre-test/post-test to demonstrate the results of the camps. Depending on the camps chosen, a published behavioral test could be completed (such as the Disruptive Behavior Rating Scale/DBRS-T or BASC), or a self-made instrument (weekly progress note or behavior log) could be used.

Although these camps can be costly to operate (depending on the number of participants and your agency), you can consider looking into grant funding from community foundations, local agencies, and state agencies. Local businesses may also be willing to donate some of the needed supplies. In addition, many of the supplies can be purchased inexpensively at discount stores, craft stores, home improvement stores, and crafting websites (such as www.orientaltrading.com or www.ssww.com).

Goal-setting therapeutic camp series

Recipe for success

Camp 1—First Course (Getting Excited about Goal Setting)
Camp 2—Second Course (Getting Our Goals on Paper)
Camp 3—Third Course (Maintaining Motivation by Developing Good Character)
Camp 4—Fourth Course (Making a Plan for Continued Goal Setting)
Camp 5—Dessert (Celebrating Good Behavior and Goal Achievement)

Purpose of the camps

The purpose of the therapeutic day camps is to provide children with behavioral and emotional problems with the opportunity to learn new ways of behaving and to receive rewards for good behavior while participating in five fun and therapeutic camps. While all of the camps will encourage children to develop social skills and self-esteem, the main focus of the camps will be on goal setting. Specifically, children will learn the importance of setting goals, how to break goals down in to achievable action steps, ways to stay motivated and continue working toward goals, and how to hold themselves accountable by being self-disciplined. Children will also learn to celebrate and take time to appreciate the rewards of working hard and achieving their goals. As a result of participating in the camps, children will have the opportunity to learn skills that will benefit them throughout the rest of their life.

Each camp will be set up with rotating stations during the morning portion of the camp that will teach and reinforce the theme of the camp. Below you will find detailed descriptions of the purpose, goals, and objectives of each camp and the corresponding activities. The camps will include lunch and an afternoon reward camp for children who meet the criteria and receive a certificate at the conclusion of the camp.

The purpose of the reward activities is to motivate children to actively participate in the camp. These activities include swimming, bowling, skating, and going to the movies. At the end of the summer, participants who meet the criteria and who have received certificates for participating in all four day camps will be allowed to participate in the reward ceremony and trip to a fun location (incorporate whatever is appropriate in your area). The camp leader can develop criteria for participation in the reward. Suggested criteria include participating in all camp activities, maintaining a positive attitude, showing respect for others, etc.

CAMP 1: GETTING EXCITED ABOUT GOAL SETTING

Goals/objectives

- To introduce the theme and purpose of the therapeutic day camps

- To motivate children and generate excitement for participation in the camps

- To begin preliminary goal setting and to present basic information about the goal-setting process

Camp itinerary

9:00—Opening session to explain the purpose of summer camps, receive breakfast, break into groups and receive camp T-shirts.

9:30—Station 1: Preliminary Goal Setting (p.155). This station will take place during breakfast as children arrive at camp. Children will be introduced to basic concepts of goal setting and will set an initial summer goal.

10:00—Station 2: Spirit Banner (p.156). Each child will make a spirit banner to introduce him- or herself during the Goal Setting Pep Rally at the end of camp.

10:30—Station 3: Planning for Group Cheers/Chants (p.157). Each group will make a chant or cheer to introduce their group during the Goal Setting Pep Rally.

11:00—Station 4: Banking on Goal Setting (p.158). Children will paint and decorate piggy banks to put their goals and progress checks towards goals in at each camp.

11:30—Goal Setting Pep Rally. Group and individual introductions and other activities to promote excitement and motivation for camp participation.

12:00—Lunch (grilled hot dogs, hamburgers, chips, juice).

12:30—Clean up from camp activities.

1:00—Afternoon reward activity—Swimming at the local park.

2:45—Finish swimming and get ready to go home.

Supply list

- Banners for Spirit Banner activity

- Fabric markers and decorations for banners

- CD player and kids' music for Group Cheers/Chants

- Paper and markers for Preliminary Goal Setting activity

- Piggy banks

- Paint for piggy banks

- Sticks for Goal Progress Check (rounded wooden sticks approx. 12 inches/30 centimeters in length)

- Breakfast bars and juice, fruit-flavored sports drink

- Food for lunch (meat, buns, chips, condiments)

- Plates, cups and forks

- Paper towels/toilet paper

- Charcoal and lighter fluid

- Aluminum foil

- Hand sanitizer

- Garbage bags

CAMP 2: GETTING OUR GOALS ON PAPER

Goals/objectives

- To become more committed to goal setting by writing goals and signing a commitment to strive to achieve goals

- To understand the importance of giving and receiving emotional support and encouragement concerning the pursuit of goals

- To learn the importance of taking responsibility for the choices and decisions in our lives

Camp itinerary

9:00—Camp introduction, break into groups, and distribute breakfast.

9:00—Station 1: Checking in on progress toward summer goals—Goal Progress Check (p.159). This station will take place during breakfast as children are arriving at the camp. Each camp will include a check-in station where a therapist will talk with children about the progress made toward his or her goal.

9:30—Station 2: Positive Parachute (p.160). Each group will design and decorate a parachute and participate in a teamwork activity.

10:15—Station 3: Poster Goal Commitment (p.161). Each child will write his goal on poster paper, sign a commitment to strive toward his or her goal, and other group members will write encouraging words on the poster.

11:00—Station 4: The Butterfly Story (p.162). The group will read and discuss the butterfly story and then make butterfly sun-catchers to remind them of the story's significance.

11:45—Lunch (pizza).

12:30—Clean up from lunch and activities.

1:00—Reward trip to the movies.

Supply list

- Goal Progress Sticks
- Rewards for those making progress toward goals
- Posters
- Markers and decorations for posters
- Butterfly sun-catchers
- Paint
- Paint brushes
- Enough copies of The Butterfly Story Handout
- Breakfast bars

- Juice
- Hand sanitizer
- Plates
- Pizza
- Drinks
- Cups
- Napkins
- Garbage bags
- Parachutes
- Goal tree and paperclips for goal tree

CAMP 3: MAINTAINING MOTIVATION BY DEVELOPING GOOD CHARACTER

Goals/objectives

- To understand the importance of developing good character traits in achieving goals

- To identify ways to develop good social skills and high self-esteem

- To connect success and goal achievement with positive character traits

Camp itinerary

9:00—Camp introduction. Break into groups and distribute breakfast.

9:00—Station 1: Checking in on progress toward summer goals—Goal Progress Check (p.159). This station will take place during breakfast as children arrive. Each camp will include a check-in station where a therapist will talk with children about the progress made toward his or her goal.

9:30—Station 2: Sticks and Stones (p.164). This activity focuses on the importance of treating others with respect and speaking kind words to others.

10:15—Station 3: Mirror, Mirror (p.165). This activity focuses on developing self-esteem and positive feelings of self-worth.

11:00—Station 4: Excellent Egg Relay Race (p.166). Children will participate in an egg relay to learn the importance of positive words and team encouragement.

11:45—Lunch (grilled hamburgers, hot dogs, chips).

12:30—Clean up from lunch and activities.

1:00—Afternoon reward (swimming at local park).

2:45—Get ready to go home.

Supply list

- Goal Progress Sticks
- Rewards for those making progress toward goals
- Sticks
- Paint
- Adhesive rhinestones
- Paint
- Paint brushes
- Mirrors with plastic backs
- Breakfast
- Juices
- Aluminum foil
- Supplies for lunch food (charcoal, lighter fluid, meat, buns, chips)
- Condiments
- Hand sanitizer
- Garbage bags
- Napkins
- Drinks
- Icepops
- Plastic eggs
- Spoons
- Goal tree and paperclips for goal tree

CAMP 4: MAKING A PLAN FOR CONTINUED GOAL SETTING

Goals/objectives

- To prepare participants for independent goal setting

- To reinforce the skills from the previous camps

- To emphasize the importance of breaking goals into manageable steps

Camp itinerary

9:00—Camp Introduction. Break into groups and receive breakfast.

9:00—Station 1: Checking in on progress toward summer goal—Goal Progress Check (p.159). This activity will take place while children are arriving and eating breakfast. Each camp will include a check-in station where a therapist will talk with children about the progress made toward his or her goal.

9:30—Station 2: Dream Catchers (p.167). This activity will focus on the importance of positive thinking and letting go of negativity when working toward goals.

10:15—Station 3: Action Steps Windsocks (p.168). This activity will focus on breaking long-term goals into achievable steps and on helping children develop skills to benefit them in future goal setting.

11:00—Station 4: Bead Bowl (p.169). This activity will allow children to create necklaces and bracelets with meaningful words to remember the goal-setting experience.

11:45—Lunch.

12:15—Clean up from lunch and activities.

1:00—Reward activity (bowling).

Supply list

- Goal Progress Sticks

- Rewards for those making progress toward goals

- Dream catcher materials

- Windsocks

- Paint

- Paint brushes

- Breakfast

- Juice

- Fast-food take-out meal

- Garbage bags

- Hand sanitizer

- Napkins

- Paper towels

- Goal tree and paperclips for tree

CAMP 5: CELEBRATING GOOD BEHAVIOR AND GOAL ACHIEVEMENT

Goals/objectives

- To reward good behavior and successful goal achievement

- To teach children to celebrate successes

- To reinforce topics from the previous camps

Camp itinerary

9:00—Camp Introduction. Break into groups, receive breakfast and reward T-shirts.
9:30—Good Behavior Ceremony (receive rewards for maintaining good behavior at camps).
10:00—Goal Achievement Ceremony (receive certificates for achieving summer goal—see pp.170–171).
11:00—Lunch (sandwiches, chips, and fruit).
12:00—Reward trip.
2:45—Clean up and get ready to go home.

Supply list

- Breakfast

- Juices

- T-shirts

- Enough good behavior rewards

- Enough goal achievement certificates

- Lunch supplies (sandwiches, chips, fruit, drinks)

- Plates

- Napkins

- Garbage bags

- Aluminum foil

- Hand sanitizer

- Cups

Activities

PRELIMINARY GOAL SETTING (CAMP 1)

Materials needed

- Goal Progress Sticks
- Markers
- Paint
- Tape

Purpose of the activity

- To help camp participants identify a summer goal
- To assist camp participants in turning to goal into manageable steps
- To explain the process of Goal Progress Sticks, the goal check-in station, and rewards for goal achievement

Description of the activity

At this station, the leader will use goal guidelines (see pp.172–174) to assist camp participants in identifying an achievable goal for the summer (during the eight-week camp period). The leader will also help participants take the overall goal and turn it into several smaller goals to achieve during each two-week period between the camps. Each camper will be given a Goal Progress Stick to decorate. The stick will be divided into sections based on the number of steps to be achieved toward his or her goal. At each of the following camps, there will be a goal check-in station. During the goal check-in station, the leader will tape off a section of the goal progress stick to denote completion of that phase of the summer goal. If progress has not been made toward the goal, the leader will encourage the child to continue working.

SPIRIT BANNER (CAMP 1)

Materials needed

- Banners
- Fabric paint
- Glitter
- Adhesive rhinestones

Purpose of the activity

- To introduce self to group in a fun way
- To become familiar with other participants in the camps
- To promote excitement for camp theme and activities

Description of the activity

Each child will be given a felt banner to decorate using fabric paint, rhinestones, glitter, and other materials. The banners are to reflect each individual child and can include his or her name, favorite colors, shapes, and other symbols. Each child will use his or her banner to introduce him- or herself to the group. These banners may also be used during the group cheer or chant.

GROUP CHEERS/CHANTS (CAMP 1)

Materials needed

- Completed banners

Purpose of the activity

- To promote teamwork and cooperation between group members

- To introduce groups and the camp theme in a fun, exciting manner

- To give camp participants the opportunity to meet other camp participants

Description of the activity

During the morning portion of the camp, each group will develop a group cheer or chant to introduce their group to the other camp participants. The cheer or chant will also incorporate the camp theme of goal setting. At the end of the morning portion of the camp, there will be a Goal Setting Pep Rally. During the pep rally, each group will perform their cheer or chant for the other groups. The groups with the most creative chants or cheers will receive a group reward.

BANKING ON GOAL SETTING (CAMP 1)

Materials needed

- Piggy banks
- Paint
- Paper/pens

Purpose of the activity

- To increase commitment toward goals for the summer
- To teach the importance of patience and perseverance

Description of the activity

Each child will be given a piggy bank to decorate (see illustration). The group leader will discuss the concept of patience and working toward a goal. If the piggy bank were emptied daily, would any money ever accumulate? How does the money in the piggy bank add up? The group leader will then ask each child to write his or her goal on a piece of paper and put it into the piggy bank. This will encourage commitment and dedication to achieving the summer goal.

GOAL PROGRESS CHECK (GOAL TREE) (CAMPS 2, 3 AND 4)

Materials needed

- Trellis
- Pot with soil to hold the trellis in place
- Paper cut into small squares with a hole punched at the top
- Paperclips or other material to clip the name to the trellis
- Prizes for the goal tree raffle

Purpose of activity

- To encourage and/or reward children for progress toward his or her summer goal
- To provide accountability for working toward the goal
- To provide a visual representation of progress toward goal achievement

Description of the activity

In order to promote accountability and responsibility, each camp will include a goal progress check station. During this station, the leader will discuss each person's progress and will request group feedback and encouragement from other camp participants. If the participant has made the predetermined amount of progress toward his or her goal, the child will be allowed to write his or her name on the square paper and attach it to the goal tree. At the end of each camp, a staff member will be blindfolded and will pull names off of the goal tree. These children will receive prizes. The names placed on the tree will remain throughout the camp to increase the odds of those children winning a prize and to encourage continued work toward goals. If participants did not make the predetermined amount of progress, they will receive encouragement from the group and suggestions for different approaches.

POSITIVE PARACHUTE (CAMP 2)

Materials needed

- Parachutes
- Paint
- Paint brushes

Purpose of the activity

- To use teamwork and creativity to decorate a group parachute
- To learn ways to encourage and cooperate with others
- To learn ways to relax and have fun

Description of the activity

The group leader will explain that the group is going to decorate a parachute using positive phrases and symbols. The parachute will "belong" to the whole group and should represent all group members. After the parachute is decorated, the group members will play a few short games that will encourage teamwork and the use of encouraging words to the other group members.

POSTER GOAL COMMITMENT (CAMP 2)

Materials needed

- Posters
- Markers

Purpose of the activity

- To write goals on paper in order to increase the level of commitment and personalization of the goal
- To receive support and encouragement from other group members and to provide support to others
- To create a visual representation of the goal each participant has set

Description of the activity

Each participant will be given a poster on which to write and draw pictures of his or her goal and what achieving the goal will look like at the end of the summer (see illustration). At the bottom of the poster, there will be a signature line for each participant to sign and commit to try his or her best to achieve the goal he or she has set. Once this has been completed, the leader and other participants will write words of support on the poster (such as "You can do it!" and "I believe in you!"). Each child will then have a visual picture of his or her goal with messages of support from peers and the group leader.

THE BUTTERFLY STORY (CAMP 2)

Materials needed

- Copies of The Butterfly Story Handout
- Butterfly sun-catchers
- Paint
- Paint brushes

Purpose of the activity

- To identify the importance of making careful choices and decisions
- To learn to take responsibility for actions
- To develop problem-solving and discussion skills

Description of the activity

The group leader will read The Butterfly Story (see handout) with the group and discuss the important concepts of the story, which include personal responsibility, careful decisions, and the need to develop good problem-solving skills. After reviewing the story concepts and relating these concepts to goal setting, group participants will paint a butterfly sun-catcher to remind them of the important concepts of the story. The Butterfly Story activity and the Poster Goal Commitment activity are designed to show the balance between needing support from others and taking personal responsibility as related to goal setting.

The Butterfly Story Handout

THE BUTTERFLY STORY (A HASSIDIC PROVERB)[1]

A long time ago, there was an old rabbi who loved to teach. He had taught for so many generations that he could hardly remember them all. This old rabbi enjoyed teaching the alphabet to little children, but he was actually famous for one thing, he was known as a mind reader. Everyone believed in his powers and no one ever doubted them.

One day, when the man was very old, a child named Moishe decided to challenge him. Moishe began to think of ways to disprove the rabbi's powers. He thought and thought, pacing back and forth until his feet carved a path in the ground. Finally, he had an idea. He would go to the field and catch a butterfly. Then, holding it in his hands, he would run to the old man and ask him, "Rabbi, what do I have in my hands?" He was quite sure the rabbi would say "a butterfly." He would ask the rabbi, "Is it alive or dead?" If the rabbi said it was dead, then Moishe would open his hand and let the butterfly fly away. But if he said it was alive, he would squeeze the butterfly between his hands and show the dead butterfly to the rabbi.

With this brilliant idea he ran to the field to catch a butterfly. Sure enough, when you look for something and you really want to find it, you will succeed. And so in no time at all, Moishe had a butterfly in his hands, and breathlessly ran to the rabbi.

The old man was sleepy when Moishe came into the room. The boy held the butterfly in his hands, tried not to squeeze it, nor to giggle as it tickled his hands, and asked the first question. "Rabbi, what do I have in my hands?" The old man began to think and after a while said, "A butterfly, my son, a butterfly." Moishe was pleased and with shining eyes he asked, "Is it dead or alive?" The old man closed his eyes and stroked his long, white beard. This time he thought for a long time. When at last he opened his eyes he said in a soft voice, "It's all in your hands, my son, it's all in your hands…"

---

1   First published in Lahad, M. (2000) *Creative Supervision: The Use of Expressive Arts Methods in Supervision and Self-supervision*. Jessica Kingsley Publishers: London.

STICKS AND STONES (CAMP 3)

Materials needed

- Sticks
- Adhesive rhinestones
- Paint

Purpose of the activity

- To understand the power of words and showing kindness and respect for others
- To develop social skills and self-esteem
- To identify coping skills and positive-thinking techniques

Description of the activity

The leader will discuss the traditional "sticks and stone" saying with the group. The group will discuss the ways in which words can hurt and how they can help others. They will identify ways to deal with hurtful words and ways to encourage positive thinking in themselves and others. Each participant will then receive a stick. The group members will paint and decorate the sticks to take home to remind them of the importance of using kind words and treating others with respect—see illustration.

MIRROR, MIRROR (CAMP 3)

Materials needed

- Mirrors with plastic backs and handles
- Paint markers

Purpose of the activity

- To develop self-esteem and self-acceptance
- To promote positive thinking
- To identify and learn self-care strategies for dealing with stressful situations

Description of the activity

The leader will discuss the importance of self-esteem and showing positive regard for ourselves. In addition, the leader will discuss with the group ways to deal with the stressful times in life and the times when it does not appear we are making any progress towards our goals. Self-care strategies will be identified and discussed. Each group member will be given a mirror with a plastic back and handle. He or she will paint the plastic side with positive thoughts and symbols (see illustration). The mirror will be a reminder to treat the person in the reflection with kindness and self-care.

EXCELLENT EGG RELAY RACE (CAMP 3)

Materials needed

- Plastic eggs
- Plastic spoons
- Prizes

Purpose of the activity

- To learn social skills and teamwork by participating in a group activity
- To learn and use positive and encouraging phrases toward group members
- To have fun while learning therapeutic skills

Description of the activity

Groups will be teams for the relay race. Plastic eggs and spoons will be used. All of the group members will have a turn to run with the egg on the spoon while trying not to drop it before reaching the next team member. The team to finish first will be the winners. Each group member will be encouraged to use positive words toward his or her teammates as well as the members of the other teams. The station leaders will also be looking for individuals exhibiting good sportsmanship to receive prizes. (The participants will not be aware of the station leader looking for good sportsmanship until the end of the activity.)

DREAM CATCHERS (CAMP 4)

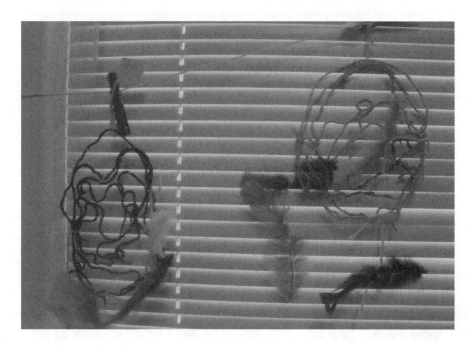

Materials needed

- Yarn
- Glitter
- Glue
- Feathers
- String

Purpose of the activity

- To believe in self and abilities
- To learn to focus on the positive and release the negative
- To learn about another culture

Description of the activity

Dream catchers were traditionally used by Native Americans and were thought to catch the good dreams while letting the bad dreams pass through the holes of the dream catcher (see illustration). The group leader will discuss the symbolism of dream catchers as related to goal setting. The group will discuss ways to let go of negativity in their lives, how to use constructive criticism, and positive-thinking techniques. Group members will then create a dream catcher to remind them of these concepts.

ACTION STEPS WINDSOCKS (CAMP 4)

Materials needed

- Windsocks (plastic ones or make them out of construction paper/card)
- Paint
- Paint brushes

Purpose of the activity

- To learn and implement a technique for dividing a large goal into achievable steps
- To increase self-efficacy and belief in abilities
- To encourage continued goal setting

Description of the activity

The group leader will discuss reasons for continuing goal setting with the group. The group will also identify reasons why some individuals achieve their goals while some individuals are not able to achieve them. The leader will then assist each group member in developing action steps in the process of achieving their goal. Each group member will receive a windsock (similar to a windchime but made of canvas or paper with long strips). The participant may paint or decorate the top of the windsock as he or she chooses and then write the action steps on the bottom pieces of the windsocks.

Variation of the activity

- Paper Action Steps Windsocks—Create the Action Steps Windsocks by having each participant cut a rectangle and four strips from colored paper. Allow participants to decorate the rectangle and write their action steps on the strips. Create a cylinder shape with the rectangle by attaching the corners and gluing together. Attach the strips to the bottom of the cylinder using glue (or punch holes and attach with yarn). Then punch three holes at the top of the cylinder, cut three strands of yarn, and attach one strand of yarn to each hole. Connect the three strands of yarn at the top so that the windsock can hang from the ceiling if desired. Share and discuss Action Steps Windsocks when complete.

BEAD BOWL (CAMP 4)

Materials needed

- Beads
- Cord

Purpose of the activity

- To develop patience while learning new techniques and skills
- To develop social skills and self-esteem
- To learn about therapeutic topics by participating in a fun activity

Description of the activity

Each child will have the opportunity to make braided key chains, bracelets, and necklaces using beads and cord. The children will be encouraged to make gifts for others and to take time to make unique and creative pieces. The group leader will relate this to goal setting because often the most worthwhile goals take patience and dedication to achieve.

GOOD BEHAVIOR AND GOAL ACHIEVEMENT CEREMONY (CAMP 5)

Materials needed

- Enough certificates
- Reward bags

Purpose of the activity

- To recognize and reward participants for good behavior and goal achievement
- To encourage future successes and motivate participants for continued goal setting
- To conclude camps with a positive event

Description of the activity

Participants will be recognized and will receive a certificate and reward for their good behavior and/or goal achievement. Participants will be praised for their hard work throughout the camps.

✓

CERTIFICATE OF ACHIEVEMENT

THIS CERTIFICATE RECOGNIZES

....

(NAME)

FOR ACHIEVING HIS/HER GOAL.

CONGRATULATIONS!

YOUR HARD WORK PAID OFF!

PRESENTED BY ....

DATE...

Handouts and forms for goal setting with children at camps

THERAPEUTIC CAMP–GOAL CRITERIA

I find it fascinating that most people plan their vacations with better care than they plan their lives. Perhaps it's because escape is easier than change.

Jim Rohn[2]

Rationale for goal setting as the therapeutic camp theme

- Children from low socioeconomic backgrounds tend to set goals that are either too low or too high. This can lead to underachievement, continuation of inter-generational poverty, and discouragement.

- Children do not typically set goals for themselves.

- Only two percent of the United States population plans for and writes down specific goals.

- However, people who write down their goals are 80 percent more likely to achieve them.

- Setting goals is an important life skill and leads to higher achievement in school and on the playing field, increased living skills, and higher self-confidence.

Summer goals: Each child will set a goal for the summer as part of the Therapeutic Camp Process. They should have a preliminary idea of the goal before the first camp.

Goal criteria

- Goals will be achievable. The purpose of the camps is to give children a chance to set a goal and to achieve it. It is better to start small and give them an experience of reaching a goal than to set a big goal that will be very difficult for them to achieve. Many of these children have already had numerous experiences of failing to reach goals. While we do want them to work for the goal, we don't want it to be so hard that they will be unmotivated and give up.

- Consider each child and assist him or her in setting a goal that is appropriate and individualized for him or her. However, remember that the goal must be something the child wants to improve. It is the *child's* goal, not ours. Children will not be motivated to work toward the goal if it is not something they want to achieve.

- Goals should be measurable. At each camp, there will be a goal check-in station. The child must have a goal that can be tracked over the course of the summer. Goals will be broken down into action steps that can be tracked at each camp. Progress will be praised and/or rewarded. Lack of progress will be discussed and an action plan for the next camp will be developed.

- State goals in the positive. (For example: "Use appropriate language" versus "Don't swear".)

Examples of appropriate goals for summer camps

These are just examples to give you ideas. Please remember that each child's goal should be individualized and appropriate for him or her.

EXAMPLE 1

Summer goal: To attend Splashdown trip at the end of the summer.

Baseline: Identify current behaviors and attendance issues that will impact attending the reward trip.

Action steps for Camp 1

- Attend day treatment at least 9 out of 10 days (tracked daily on attendance chart).
- Receive at least 90 percent happy faces[3] for group behavior (tracked daily based on group and individual behavior plan).

Reward for achieving action steps for Camp 1

- Participation in Reward Event at Camp 2.
- Prize to use during Reward Event (swim toys, goggles, etc.).

EXAMPLE 2

Summer goal: To use appropriate language during 95 percent of the time in the group (appropriate language will be specifically defined).

Baseline: Currently uses swearwords and vulgar language on average ten times daily.

Action steps for Camp 1

- Reduce swearing from an average of ten times a day to an average of six to eight by Camp 2 (tracked using a behavior chart, initialed and signed daily by the child and therapist).
- When angry, pause for five seconds and breath deeply to reduce impulsive outbursts (also tracked using behavior chart).

Reward for achieving action steps for Camp 1

- Individual time with therapist receiving praise and encouragement.
- 20 minutes of "free" time in group to engage in an enjoyable activity.

---

3   Each day a child could receive a happy face for great behavior, a straight face for okay behavior, or a frowning face for problem behavior during group time.

Example 3

Summer goal: To take responsibility for self by identifying personal behaviors of self that contributed to an issue on four out of five occasions.

Baseline: Currently accepts responsibility for actions on one out of five occasions (20 percent of the time).

Action steps for Camp 1

- Identify personal behaviors that lead to conflicts on average of 40 percent of the time during the two weeks between Camp 1 and Camp 2 (tracked using behavior chart for Circle Time, when all of the members of the group meet together with the group leader and have group discussions, and other conflicts that arise during the day). The group leader will discuss progress and issues daily with the child.

- Child will read four short stories of conflicts (as selected by therapist and/or the goal leader) and identify the actions of both people in the story that lead to the conflict. The group leader will discuss and document completion of this action step with the child.

Rewards for achieving action steps for Camp 1

- One free "Caught Being Good" coupon.

Goal Setting Worksheet

Child's name: . . . . Age:. . . . .

Group: . . . .

Goal check-in leader: . . . .

Goal I want to work on this summer:

. . . .

What I think I need to do to achieve my goal:

. . . .

Action steps for Camp 1:

. . . .

Reward for achieving action steps for Camp 1:

. . . .

Action steps for Camp 2:

. . . .

Reward for achieving action steps for Camp 2:

. . . .

Action steps for Camp 3:

. . . .

Reward for achieving action steps for Camp 3:

. . . .

Action steps for Camp 4:

. . . .

✓

Reward for achieving action steps for Camp 4:

. . . .

Examples of prizes or rewards I would like if I achieve my overall summer goal are:

. . . .

By signing below, I am agreeing to:

- work to achieve my goal
- be honest with my goal leader, my therapist, and myself about my progress
- remember that I am only competing against myself with my goal setting. I am doing my personal best
- remember that progress takes time and to not give up when it does not seem like I am going to achieve my goal
- the goal I listed above being something that I want to improve and am willing to work toward
- believe I can achieve my goal.

Signature of commitment: . . . .

Date: . . . .

Goal leader's signature: . . . .

Date: . . . .

Goal Leader Information

1. The main purpose of the goal leader is to encourage/motivate the children and provide another level of accountability to the goal-setting process.

2. The leader for each group will bring the group to you as they arrive at the camp. You will then have a chance to talk with the children and see if they are making progress toward their goals. You will have to rely on the information from the child and group leader to determine if progress is being made.

3. Children who are making progress will be given a card to write their name on and put on the goal tree for the opportunity to have their name selected to receive a prize at the end of the camp (see Goal Progress Check activity on p.159). All children making progress toward their goals will also receive a special snack at the end of the camp.

4. Children who are not making progress toward their goal will be encouraged by the goal leader.

5. You will have a binder to keep all of the information on each child in your goal check-in group. Please keep up with the binder and make a note of whether the child was making progress toward his or her goal at each camp. We will use this as measurable data so it is very important that you keep up with it and return it at the end of summer.

Your assigned groups are:

Ideas for adapting goal-setting camp activities to other settings

Many of the activities from the camp itineraries are easily adaptable to other settings such as group counseling, day-treatment programs, and character education programs. The schedule given immediately below is ideal for a group that meets daily for one hour. However, this schedule and curriculum could easily be extended as needed for groups that do not meet every day. For example, groups that meet twice a week could adjust the schedule so that they are completing two of the activities each week and continue with the curriculum until all of the activities are complete. Groups that meet for longer periods of time (two-hour sessions) might consider completing two activities per meeting.

There are some advantages to using this curriculum in a group setting as opposed to a camp setting:

- First, the group members will meet more regularly. This will allow rapport to develop and group members to benefit from relationships with each other and the group leader.

- In addition, the group members will have more group time to work on their goals and more accountability from other group members and the group leader about their progress and commitment to their goals.

- Finally, the more consistent meeting schedule and extended time period will allow the group members more time to absorb the curriculum, achieve goals, and learn goal-setting skills that will benefit them in the future.

SAMPLE WEEKLY SCHEDULE FOR GOAL-SETTING CURRICULUM AND ACTIVITIES

(Detailed descriptions and instructions for the activities are available on pp.155–170.)

Week 1: Introduction to goal setting

MONDAY: INTRODUCTION AND SPIRIT BANNERS

Give group members an overview of the curriculum and activities for the next few weeks. Provide group members with the supplies to decorate the spirit banners. As the group members are completing the project, discuss ideas for goals and allow each group member to begin thinking of a goal that he or she would like to achieve over the next few weeks.

TUESDAY: PRELIMINARY GOAL SETTING WORKSHEETS

Give each group member a copy of the Goal Setting Worksheet. Discuss the importance of setting achievable goals and making a commitment to work toward reaching the goal. Assist members in developing goals, determining ways to track progress (behavior logs, etc.), and in completing the worksheet.

WEDNESDAY: COMPLETE WORKSHEETS AND DEVELOP MOTIVATING CHANTS/CHEERS

If needed, assist group members in completing and signing their Goal Setting Worksheets. As a group, develop some motivating cheers, chants, and dances to encourage members to work toward their goals. Allow the group members to write the chants and cheers on large paper or posters and display in the group room.

THURSDAY: BANKING ON GOAL SETTING

Complete the Banking on Goal Setting activity—see p.158.

FRIDAY: GOAL SETTING PEP RALLY AND INTRODUCTION OF THE GOAL TREE

Have a pep rally to motivate the group members to work on their goals and complete the goal-setting activities. Let the group members present their spirit banners to the group and tell the other group members about their goal. As a group, say the chants and cheers that were developed earlier in the week. Have the goal tree set up and explain that each day group members who are making progress toward their goals will get to add their name to the goal tree. At the end of the week, names will be pulled from the tree and the group members whose names were pulled will receive small prizes. If possible, have special snacks available and make the pep rally a fun day. Remind the group members that goal setting and goal achievement require hard work, but it is also important to celebrate and encourage one another throughout the process.

Week 2: Getting our goals on paper

MONDAY: REVIEW GOALS, METHOD OF TRACKING GOALS, AND BEGIN POSTER GOAL
COMMITMENT ACTIVITY

Begin by asking every group member to state his or her goal and how he or she will track progress toward the goal (typically by use of a behavior log). Explain that beginning at the next group session, the members will check in and discuss progress toward their goals. Members who are making progress will add a card with their name on it to the goal tree daily. Explain that this week's sessions will focus on increasing commitment to their goals. After the review of the goals, give each member a piece of poster or card (16 x 20 inches/40 x 50 centimeters is a great size). Ask each group member to write his or her goal on the poster and decorate it. Keep the posters until the next group session when they will be completed.

TUESDAY: GOAL PROGRESS CHECK-IN AND COMPLETE POSTER GOAL COMMITMENT ACTIVITY

Begin by allowing each group member time to verbalize his or her progress toward the goal and any challenges that he or she is facing in working on the goal. Allow members who are making progress (based on self-report and data from behavior logs) to add their name to the goal tree. Encourage members who are having difficulty and assist them in developing strategies for addressing the challenges of working toward their goals. Distribute the goal posters from the previous session. Group members will write words of encouragement on each member's poster (see the Poster Goal Commitment activity, p.161, for a more detailed description). If possible, display these in the group room or allow members to take them home to provide encouragement outside of the group setting.

WEDNESDAY: GOAL PROGRESS CHECK-IN AND THE BUTTERFLY STORY ACTIVITY

Begin by repeating the goal progress check-in described for Tuesday's session. This format will be used to begin each session. After this is complete distribute copies of The Butterfly Story (see The Butterfly Story activity, p.162, for copies of the story and the activity description). As a group, discuss the story and how it relates to goal setting (particularly to choosing our actions and accepting responsibility for the choices we make). Assist each group member in identifying some specific ways to achieve his or her goals and to take responsibility for goal progress.

THURSDAY: GOAL PROGRESS CHECK-IN AND THE BUTTERFLY STORY ACTIVITY

Begin with the goal check-in and goal-tree procedure. Review The Butterfly Story with the group and distribute materials needed to make butterfly sun-catchers. Explain that the sun-catcher will serve to remind the group member of the lessons from The Butterfly Story. Allow group members to take the sun-catchers home with them (once they are dry).

FRIDAY: GOAL PROGRESS CHECK-IN, REWARDS AND THE POSITIVE PARACHUTE ACTIVITY

Begin with the goal progress check-in and goal-tree procedure. Complete the positive parachute activity (see Positive Parachute activity, p.160, for description). Consider having the group name written in the middle of the parachute and then asking each group member to write his or her goal on the sections of the parachute. If possible, take the parachute outside and play some simple team-building games with it (e.g. everyone shaking the parachute with their right hand, having two members run under the parachute and switch places, etc.). The parachute can be kept by the group leader and used for various future activities. At the end of the group session, blindfold a group member and have him or her pull a designated number of names from the goal tree. Give the members whose names were pulled small prizes. Encourage all group members to continue working toward their goals.

Week 3: Maintaining motivation by developing good character

MONDAY: GOAL PROGRESS CHECK-IN AND BEGIN THE STICKS AND STONES ACTIVITY

Begin with the goal progress check-in and goal-tree procedure. Explain to group members that this week will focus on developing good character in order to maintain motivation. In order to experience continued success with goal setting, good character traits such as belief in self and others, kindness, cooperation, and perseverance are needed. Begin the Sticks and Stones activity (see the activity description, p.164, for more details). Be sure to discuss the impact of words and the power that words have to hurt us or to encourage us.

TUESDAY: GOAL PROGRESS CHECK-IN AND COMPLETE THE STICKS AND STONES ACTIVITY

Begin with the goal progress check-in and goal-tree procedure. Review and complete the Sticks and Stones activity.

WEDNESDAY: GOAL CHECK-IN AND BEGIN THE MIRROR, MIRROR ACTIVITY

Begin with the goal progress check-in and goal-tree procedure. Explain the Mirror, Mirror activity (see the activity description, p.165, for more details) and discuss the significance of the mirrors (particularly that the way we feel about ourselves can influence our goal progress and achievement). If time allows, distribute materials and begin the activity.

THURSDAY: GOAL CHECK-IN AND COMPLETE THE MIRROR, MIRROR ACTIVITY

Begin with the goal progress check-in and goal-tree procedure. Review the Mirror, Mirror activity from the previous session and allow group members to complete their mirrors. When the mirrors are dry, group members may take them home as a reminder of the lessons of the activity.

FRIDAY: GOAL CHECK-IN, REWARDS, AND THE EXCELLENT EGG RELAY RACE ACTIVITY

Begin with the goal progress check-in and goal-tree procedure. Spend some time discussing how group members feel about their goals, their progress toward their goals, and challenges in making progress toward their goals. Discuss ideas and strategies for dealing with the challenges as a group. Complete the egg relay (see p.166) and discuss the importance of teamwork and cooperation. At the end of the session, blindfold one of the group members and have him or her pull a designated number of names from the goal tree. Distribute small prizes to the members whose names were pulled out and encourage all members to keep working toward their goals.

Week 4: Making a plan for continued goal setting

MONDAY: GOAL CHECK-IN AND BEGIN THE DREAM CATCHERS ACTIVITY

Begin with the goal progress check-in and goal-tree procedure. Explain that this week will focus on helping group members make a plan for continued goal setting outside of the group. Discuss the Dream Catcher activity (see the activity description, p.167, for more details) and begin to make dream catchers if time allows.

TUESDAY: GOAL CHECK-IN AND COMPLETE THE DREAM CATCHERS ACTIVITY

Begin with the goal progress check-in and goal-tree procedure. Review and complete the Dream Catcher activity.

WEDNESDAY: GOAL CHECK-IN AND BEGIN THE ACTION STEPS WINDSOCKS ACTIVITY

Begin with the goal progress check-in and goal-tree procedure. Explain the Action Steps Windsocks activity (see the activity description, p.168, for more details) and assist group members in identifying action steps in the goal-setting process. If time allows, begin to decorate the windsocks.

THURSDAY: GOAL CHECK-IN AND COMPLETE THE ACTION STEPS WINDSOCKS ACTIVITY

Begin with the goal progress check-in and goal-tree procedures. Review and complete the Action Steps Windsocks activity.

FRIDAY: GOAL CHECK-IN, REWARDS, AND THE BEAD BOWL ACTIVITY

Begin with the goal progress check-in and goal-tree procedure. Explain to the group that this is the last group session before the Goal Achievement Ceremony. Discuss the Bead Bowl activity (see the activity description, p.169, for more details) and assist each group member in identifying a word that will remind him of goal setting when he is away from the group. Allow the group members to create beaded jewelry with words that remind them of the importance of goal setting. At the end of the session, blindfold a group member and ask him or her to pull a designated number of names from the goal tree. Give each of these members small prizes and remind all members about the ceremony at the next session.

Week 5: Celebrating goal achievement

MONDAY: GOAL ACHIEVEMENT CEREMONY

Begin by summarizing the sessions from the past few weeks and the progress that each member has made toward his or her goal. Provide all members who completed the sessions with a Certificate of Completion (see p.241). Recognize each of the group members that achieved their goal by giving them a certificate and a small prize. After the ceremony is complete, have a party with special snacks, or arrange for the group to complete a fun activity together (such as going to the bowling alley or skating rink).

Self-esteem, anger-control, and impulse-control therapeutic camp series

Making me the best I can be

Camp 1—Kick Off Summer Pep Rally
Camp 2—Anger Control/Afternoon Reward
Camp 3—Self-Esteem
Camp 4—Impulse Control/Afternoon Reward
Camp 5—Reward Camp/Closing Ceremony

Purpose of the camps

The goal of the summer camps is to provide children with emotional and behavioral problems with a fun and therapeutic environment to learn new ways of behaving and to be rewarded for good behavior. The theme for all these summer camps is "Making me the best I can be." Each of the camps will incorporate this theme into the day and will focus on a different behavior area or skill in order to encourage the participants to be the best they can be.

The first camp will be a two-hour pep rally to give the children information about the camps and rewards and to motivate them to participate in the program. The next three camps will be set up with rotating stations that relate to the theme of the day. The three themes for the camps will be anger control, self-esteem, and impulse control. The anger-control and impulse-control camps will include an afternoon reward (the criteria that must be met in order to receive the reward are listed on p.185 and p.189). The final camp of the summer will include a graduation and award ceremony in the morning and a reward trip in the afternoon for children who have participated in all camps and meet other criteria (see p.191).

The children and the group leader will each complete a survey at the first camp and fourth camp in an attempt to determine the impact of the camps on the child's behavior. Objectives, goals, and activities for each camp are described in the itineraries given below.

CAMP 1: KICK OFF SUMMER PEP RALLY

Goals/objectives

- To provide children with information about the summer camps

- To motivate children to participate in the camps

- To encourage participants to develop appropriate behaviors and self-esteem

Camp itinerary

12:00—Opening ceremony for Summer Programs. Explain the purpose and theme of the camps (making me the best I can be) and the rewards for participating in the camps.
12:15—Skits/Dances/Introductions of each group participating in the camps to encourage the participants to develop self-esteem and impulse control.
1:00—Staff skit to introduce staff members and reiterate the theme of the summer camps.
1:20—Throwing out balls (printed with "Making me the best I can be")/other prizes.
1:40—Snacks (ice-cream, etc.) and free time.
2:00—Get ready to go home.

Supply list

- Painted banner (for children to run through at the beginning of the camp)

- CD player and batteries (to provide music for the skits)

- 3 water-coolers (to keep children hydrated during the outdoor camp)

- 2 packages of fruit-flavored sports drink (for water-coolers)

- 300 paper napkins (for drinks and snacks)

- 200 paper cups (for drinks from water-coolers)

- 100 foam balls (to be given out during the pep rally)

- 2 packs of permanent markers (to write the camp theme on the foam balls)

CAMP 2: ANGER CONTROL/AFTERNOON REWARD

Goals/objectives

- To demonstrate and assist participants in developing new and healthier ways to manage anger

- To assist participants in gaining insight about themselves and the way that they currently manage anger

- To provide the participants with examples of appropriate ways to handle stress, tension, and other situations that may trigger anger outbursts

Camp itinerary

9:00—Opening session: Explain the purpose of the camp (to develop anger control and continue to become "the best they can be"). Participants will break into groups and have a snack during this time.

9:30—Station 1: Positive Word Wall (p.192).

10:00—Station 2: The Color of Anger (p.194).

10:30—Station 3: Animal Anger-Control Questionnaire (p.196).

11:00—Station 4: Create a Group Totem Pole (p.198) from the animal/conflict resolution styles from Station 3.

11:30—Lunch (emphasizing social skills and functional living skills).

12:15—Clean up from lunch.

12:30—Presentation of totem poles and word walls (that were developed at the above stations in individuals' groups).

1:00—Reward activity (swimming at local park).

2:45—Clean up and get ready to go home.

Criteria for receiving reward (swimming)

- Attend the camp

- Participate and complete each camp station

- Follow the rules and instructions given by camp leaders

- Display a good attitude and show respect for others throughout the day

Supply list

- Washable paint (to be used to paint the Positive Word Wall and animals for the totem pole)

- 100 animal pictures (to be decorated at the totem pole station)

- 15 wooden dowels (totems poles for the totem pole station)

- 9 sets of markers (to be used to decorate the animals for the totem pole)

- 30 clipboards (to be used during the "What type animal are you?" station)
- Masking tape (to be used to hold the word wall in place)
- 50 jumbo paint brushes (to paint the word wall)
- Large roll of paper (for the word wall)
- 120 icepops (for afternoon snack)
- 120 cereal bars (for morning snack)
- 200 paper cups (for beverages)
- 2 flavors of powdered sports drink (for water-coolers to keep participants hydrated during the outdoor camp)

CAMP 3: SELF-ESTEEM

Goals/objectives

- To promote healthy self-esteem among the camp participants by helping each participant to identify positive aspects of his or herself

- To assist the participants in gaining insight and awareness into themselves

- To encourage participants to develop a positive self-image by participating in activities that encourage self-expression and creativity

Camp itinerary

9:00—Opening session. Explain the purpose of the camp (to develop good self-esteem and to continue to become "the best they can be"). Participants will break into groups, have snacks, and receive T-shirts.

9:45—Station 1: Pull a Duck (p.200).

10:30—Station 2: Carousel Ride with cotton candy, Face Painting (p.202).

11:15—Clean up and get ready for lunch.

11:30—Lunch (emphasizing social skills and functional living skills).

12:15—Station 3: Silent and Verbal Water Balloon Toss (p.203).

1:00—Station 4: Kite Decorating and Flying (p.205).

1:45—Clean up for the day, have snack, and get ready to go home.

Supply list

- 200 balloons (for the Water Balloon Toss activity)

- 75 rubber ducks (for the Pull a Duck activity)

- 3 inflatable baby pools (for the Pull a Duck activity)

- Face-painting materials (for the Face Painting station)

- 140 blank kites (for the Kite Decorating and Flying station)

- 140 cereal bars (morning snack)

- 300 icepops (afternoon snack)

- 300 paper cups (for beverages)

- 2 flavors of powdered sports drink (for water-coolers)

- Markers/paint (for Kite Decorating station)

- Paper towels (for icepops and clean up)

- Small prizes (for the Pull a Duck activity)

Prizes for Pull a Duck

- Level 1: Participation—candy
- Level 2: Answering all questions and showing respect to others—one bag of hot chips
- Level 3: Pulling a duck with a dot on the bottom—small prizes such as yoyos, batons, etc.

Prizes for Silent and Verbal Water Balloon Toss

- Level 1: Participation—icepops
- Level 2: Winning pair from each group—ice-cream sandwiches
- Level 3: Winners in each age bracket—CD player

CAMP 4: IMPULSE CONTROL/AFTERNOON REWARD

Goals/objectives

- To help children to differentiate between positive and negative behaviors as well as to identify the consequences of both types of behaviors

- To assist clients in developing impulse control and respect for others by participating cooperatively in camp activities

- To promote healthy and creative ways to alleviate stress, express self, and release anger and tension

Camp itinerary

9:00—Opening session. Explain the purpose of the camp (to develop impulse control and to continue to become "the best they can be"). Participants will break into groups and have a snack during this time.

9:30—Station 1: Gardening (p.206).

10:15—Station 2: "Great," "Could-Be-Better," and "Unacceptable" Behavior Bean Bag Toss (p.207).

11:00—Station 3: Concrete Block/Stepping Stone (p.210).

11:45—Get ready for lunch.

12:00—Lunch (emphasizing social skills and functional living skills).

12:30—Presentation of Concrete Blocks and Stepping Stones.

1:00—Reward activity (swimming at local park).

2:45—Get ready to go home.

Criteria for receiving reward (swimming)

- Attend the camp

- Participate and complete each camp station

- Follow the rules and instructions given by camp leaders

- Display a good attitude and show respect for others throughout the day

Supply list

- 150 paper cups (for Gardening)

- 2 big bags of soil (for Gardening)

- Assorted flower seeds (for Gardening)

- 4 bags of concrete (for Concrete Blocks)

- Small stepping stones (for Stepping Stones)

- Mold pans (for Concrete Blocks)

- Alphabet raised letters (for Concrete Blocks)
- Colored stones (for Stepping Stones)
- Paint (for Stepping Stones)
- Small bean bags (for Bean Bag Toss)
- 3 large containers (for Bean Bag Toss)
- Small prizes (for Bean Bag Toss)
- 150 cereal bars (for morning snack)
- 150 icepops (for afternoon snack)
- 200 cups (for drinks during outdoor activities)
- 2 flavors of powdered sports drinks (for water-coolers)

CAMP 5: REWARD CAMP/CLOSING CEREMONY

Goals/objectives

- To provide a reward for participants who have successfully completed all therapeutic day camps

- To promote self-esteem among participants and distribute certificates of achievement for completion of the therapeutic day camps

- To give participants an opportunity to display the behaviors and skills they have learned from the camps in a social setting

Camp itinerary

9:00—Closing ceremony at a local park or outdoor setting. Distribution of Certificates of Completion and Reward Bags with T-shirts (the criteria for receiving a T-shirt are listed below).

10:15—Get ready for lunch.

10:30—Lunch.

11:30—Reward activity at a local entertainment spot, such as a waterpark, bowling alley, etc.

1:45—Get ready to go home.

Criteria for receiving certificates and T-shirts and attending the reward trip

- Attend all camps

- Complete all camp stations and activities

- Display a positive attitude and show respect to others at all camps

- Follow the rules and comply with adult requests

- Show progress toward behavior goals (as determined by group leader)

Supply list

- Certificates (to be handed out at closing ceremony—see p.212)

- Materials (t-shirts, candy, bags of chips, yoyos, bubbles, coloring books, art supplies, etc.) for reward bags (to be handed out at closing ceremony)

Activities

POSITIVE WORD WALL (CAMP 2)

Purpose of the activity

- To show participants new ways to alleviate stress and anger

- To assist participants in replacing negative self-talk with positive self-talk

- To encourage participants to exhibit anger control and show respect for others

Description of the activity

Each group will use large paper and paint to construct a positive word wall. Group members will have the opportunity to paint two positive words/pictures about themselves and each of the other members of the group on to the wall. The group leader will discuss the activity with the group using the discussion questions below. At the end of the camp, each group will present their wall to all the camp participants.

Instructions for leaders

- Leaders will begin by explaining that the group will be constructing a "positive word wall."

- Leaders will discuss with participants the types of words that are typically associated with graffiti, anger, and losing your temper (negative words). Leaders will then discuss how our thinking and the words that we speak can influence our behaviors.

- Leaders will explain to the group that they are going to make a positive word wall using positive words about themselves and the other group members.

- The leader and assistant will set up a piece of large paper and each group member will have an opportunity to paint two positive words about themselves and the other group members on the banner.

- After the activity is completed, the leader will use the discussion questions below to help the participants process the activity.

- At the end of the camp, each group will present their positive word wall to all the participants of the camp.

Discussion opportunities and ideas

Listed below are questions for the leaders to ask the participants before, during, and after the activity is completed:

- What positive words did you write on the positive word wall about yourself? Why did you choose those words?

- What positive words did you write about the other group members? Why did you choose those words?

- How did you feel after writing on the positive word wall?

- Was it easier to think of nice things about yourself or others? Why?

- Was it easier to write nice things on the paper than to say them out loud? Why?

- What did you think about this activity?

THE COLOR OF ANGER (CAMP 2)

Purpose of the the activity

- To help participants identify warning signs of extreme anger

- To help individuals identify ways to calm themselves and alleviate anger

- To assist individuals in developing healthy anger-management strategies

Description of the activity

Each group leader will begin by discussing colors and what types of feelings are associated with different colors. The leader will ask participants what color(s) they think of when they are angry and what color(s) they associate with being peaceful and calm. Leaders will go over different ways to calm and relax yourself (such as deep-breathing techniques). Group members will then have the opportunity to paint the colors as well as pictures of things that they associate with peace and happiness on the banner/positive word wall. At the end of the camp, the group members will present their banner/word wall to all camp participants.

Instructions for leaders

- The leader will begin by discussing colors and what the group members associate with different colors. The leader will also ask what colors are associated with what type of feelings (for example, red is typically associated with anger, light blues and greens are typically associated with calm and peaceful feelings).

- The leader will ask the group if they ever "see red" when they are angry and discuss with the group how certain colors and environments can help to create more anger or to calm and soothe tension.

- The leader will discuss with the group different ways to relax yourself and to alleviate anger, tension, and stress. The leader will teach his or her group a deep-breathing technique.

- Each group member will have the opportunity to paint the colors as well as pictures of things that they associate with peace and happiness on the banner/word wall.

- The group will discuss each member's colors/drawings and why the group member associates these things with peace and happiness.

Discussion opportunities and ideas

Listed below are questions for the group leader to discuss with the group before, during, and after the activity:

- What is your favorite color? Why?

- What color do you think about when you are angry?

- What color do you think about when you are happy and calm?

- What are some ways that you can calm yourself down when you are upset or stressed out?

- How did you feel after the deep-breathing activity? Could you do this yourself when you begin to feel angry?

- What pictures and colors did you draw on the banner? How can you use these things to calm yourself down when you feel upset or angry?

- What did you think about this activity?

ANIMAL ANGER-CONTROL QUESTIONNAIRE (CAMP 2)

Purpose of the activity

- To identify each participant's conflict-resolution style

- To assist each participant in gaining insight about how he or she handles conflict and deals with anger

- To identify healthy ways to resolve anger and conflict

Description of the activity

Each group leader will begin by discussing animals and anger with the group. The group leader will ask if a lion and donkey act the same way when they are angry. The leader will then explain that like animals, we are all unique and we each have different ways of dealing with anger and stress. The leader will assist the group members in completing the Animal Anger-Control Questionnaire (see pp.117–118). After the group members complete the questionnaire, the group leader will help each participant to identify the animal that has the same conflict-resolution styles as him- or herself. The group leader will then explain how each animal handles anger. The group leader will discuss with the group the pros and cons of each style, as well as appropriate ways to handle conflict resolution. The group members will then have the opportunity to paint and decorate a cut-out of the animal that corresponds with their particular conflict-resolution style.

Instructions for leaders

- The leader will begin by discussing animals and how they handle anger with the group. (How do you think a lion acts when he is angry? What about a donkey?)

- The leader will then discuss how each animal is different and handles anger and conflict in a different way. The leader will explain that humans are the same. The leader may share what type of animal he or she is on the questionnaire if desired and how he or she has learned to handle conflict and anger in appropriate ways.

- The leader will then assist each group member in completing the questionnaire and identifying which animal has the same type of conflict-resolution style as him- or herself.

- After the questionnaires are completed, the leader will discuss how each animal handles conflict and anger as well as the pros and cons of each style; for example, "the lion" conflict-resolution style acts quickly in times of stress (pro), but can be intimidating to other people (con).

- The leader will also help the members to identify appropriate ways to handle anger and stress.

- The leader will then pass out cut-outs of the different types of animals for the participants to paint and decorate.

Discussion opportunities and ideas

- How do different animals act when they are angry?

- What animal/conflict-resolution style are you?

- What are some positive things about each style? What are the negative things?

- What are some healthy ways to handle anger and stress?

- Do you think you handle anger like the animal that you matched up with? Why, or why not?

- What did you think about this activity?

CREATE A GROUP TOTEM POLE (CAMP 2)

Purpose of the activity

- To promote group unity and conflict-resolution skills

- To encourage participants to accept their differences and to respect themselves and others

- To develop social skills and self-esteem by working cooperatively on the group activity

Description of the activity

The leader will begin by asking the group members if they know what a totem pole is. The leader will explain that a totem pole is used to tell a story of a group or family and that each animal on the totem pole represents a different family member or group member. The leader will explain that the group will be making a totem pole using their animal from the Animal Anger-Control Questionnaire. The leader will explain that each individual is represented on the totem pole and that the totem pole provides a picture of the whole group. The group members will then be given the opportunity to finish decorating their animals and then to attach them to the group totem pole (see illustrations). At the end of the day, the group will present their totem pole to all the camp participants.

Instructions for leaders

- Leaders will discuss totem poles and what the totem poles represent (individual differences within a group, group unity).

- Leaders will explain that the group members are going to create a group totem pole from their individual animals from the Animal Anger-Control Questionnaire. Group members will also have the opportunity to select a different animal that they feel better represents them for the totem pole (if they desire).

- Group members will finish decorating and painting their animals.
- Group members will then attach their animals to the totem pole.
- Leaders will discuss how the totem pole represents each person as well as the group.
- At the end of the camp, each group will present their totem pole to all camp participants.

Discussion opportunities and ideas

- How does the animal on the totem pole represent you?
- How does the totem pole represent your group?
- What would your group be like if everyone was just the same?
- How do you treat people who are different to you?
- What are some ways that you can get along with others?
- What are some ways to handle conflicts in a peaceful way?
- What did you think about this activity?

PULL A DUCK (CAMP 3)

Purpose of the activity

- To assist participants in getting to know each other
- To help participants identify positive aspects of themselves
- To improve communication and listening skills

Description of the activity

This activity is a spin-off of the popular carnival or fairground game. Each participant will pull three different ducks from a small pool. Each duck will be numbered and will correspond with a different question (see questions below). The participants will answer their question and will listen and show respect while others answer their questions. At the end of the activity, all group members who participate in the activity will be allowed to select a prize.

Instructions for leaders

- At the beginning of the activity, the leader will ask if anyone has ever played the Pull a Duck game at a fair or carnival.
- The leader will tell the group that they are going to play a new version of this game.
- Each participant will pull three ducks from the pool and answer the corresponding questions.
- All participants will listen and show respect while others are talking.
- At the end of the activity, all members who participated and showed respect will be allowed to select a prize.

Questions to correspond with ducks

- What is your favorite food?
- If you could have a pet, what would you get? What would you name it?
- What are two positive things about you?
- What is your favorite movie?
- Who is your hero?
- What is your favorite color?
- If you could go anywhere in the world, where would you go?
- What do you want to be when you grow up?
- What is your favorite sport?
- If you could have any kind of car you wanted, what would you pick?
- What is your favorite subject at school?

- If you were given three wishes, what would they be?
- If you were the President, what would you do?
- What is something positive you can say about the person sitting next to you?
- What is your favorite candy?
- What are two things you like to do with your best friend?
- If you had a whole day to do whatever you wanted, what would you do?
- If you had to eat the same meal everyday for the rest of your life, what would you pick?
- What is your favorite time of year? Why?
- Where would you like to go on vacation? Why?
- If you were a teacher, what would you teach? Would you be strict or easy?
- If you could have any superpower, what would you choose?
- If you were an animal, what would you be?

CAROUSEL RIDE AND FACE PAINTING (CAMP 3)

Purpose of the activity

- To promote self-expression and creativity

- To assist participants in developing social skills and communication skills

- To develop self-esteem by participating in a fun activity

Description of the activity

Participants will have the opportunity to ride the carousel (or other fun activity) and to have their face painted. Each participant will also receive cotton candy at the carousel. Each participant will exhibit good social skills and manners while riding the carousel and waiting for a turn to get his or her face painted.

Instructions for leaders

- The leader will tell his or her group that they are going to have an opportunity to put into practice all the skills and behaviors that have been discussed ("being the best they can be," using good manners and exhibiting good social skills).

- The leader will explain to the group that they are about to participate in a fun activity that includes riding the carousel, eating cotton candy, and getting their face painted.

- The leader will watch closely as the participants complete the activities to see which group members are exhibiting good social skills and using good manners.

Discussion opportunities and ideas

Listed below are questions to discuss with the group before, during, and after the activities:

- What is the reason to use good manners?

- How do good manners and social skills help everyone?

- How can you have fun and still "be the best you can be?"

- What did you choose to get painted on your face? Why?

- What did you think about this activity?

SILENT AND VERBAL WATER BALLOON TOSS (CAMP 3)

Purpose of the activity

- To promote social skills by participating in a cooperative game
- To develop communication skills and listening skills
- To identify the reasons for good communication skills and social skills

Description of the activity

This activity is a therapeutic adaptation of the traditional water balloon toss activity. (This involves several teams of two people each. Each team is given a water balloon. The team to toss their balloon back and forth for the longest time without breaking it is the winner of the water balloon toss.) The leader will divide the group into pairs. Each group will first complete the water balloon toss *silently*. If they talk or use verbal communication, they will have to sit down for 30 seconds. The silent water balloon toss will encourage participants to pay attention to nonverbal communication. At the end of the toss, the group that has been standing up the longest and has not busted their balloon will receive a prize. After the silent water balloon toss, the same pairs will complete the water balloon toss again, but this time they will be allowed to communicate verbally. At the end of the toss, the group that has not busted their balloon will receive a prize.

Instructions for leaders

- The leader will ask if anyone has ever participated in a water balloon toss. He or she will explain that they are going to have a water balloon toss but that the first round is going to be a little different to a traditional water balloon toss.
- The leader will then divide the group into pairs and distribute the water balloons.
- He or she will explain that the group members are not allowed to talk. The partners will have to watch closely and pay attention to body language. If one of the partners talks, then the pair has to sit down for 30 seconds.
- At the end, the pair that has been seated least and busted the least balloons will receive a prize.
- After the "silent" balloon toss, the same pairs will complete the water balloon toss in the traditional way.
- The group with least busted balloons will receive a prize.
- The leader will discuss the questions below and what the group members learned from participating in this activity.
- If time allows, the leader may switch pairs and repeat the games.

Discussion opportunities and ideas

- Which was easier—verbal or nonverbal? Why?
- What did you think about the "silent" balloon toss?
- How was communication with your partner important in both types of water balloon toss?
- What are some good communication skills?
- What are some ways to show your partner that you are listening to him or her?
- What did you think about this activity?

KITE DECORATING AND FLYING (CAMP 3)

Purpose of the activity

- To develop self-esteem by painting a personal kite to represent him or herself

- To promote creativity, positive thinking, and self-expression

- To show respect for others and exhibit good social skills

Description of the activity

Each participant will have the opportunity to paint and decorate a kite to represent him- or herself. The group members will then present their kites to the group and explain how the kite represents them. After presenting their kites to the group, the leader will take the group to a separate area where they will have the opportunity to fly the kites.

Instructions for leaders

- The leader will begin by explaining to the group that they are going to make their own kites.

- The leader will tell the members that they are each unique and special and that they should paint and decorate their kites to represent themselves.

- After the group members have finished decorating their kites, each member will present his or her kite to the group and explain why it represents him or her.

- At the end of the activity, the group leader will take the group to a separate area where they will have the opportunity to fly their kites.

Discussion opportunities and ideas

- What are some ways that we are alike? What are some ways that we are different?

- How did you decide what to paint on your kite?

- Does everyone's kite look alike? Why?

- What are three positive things about you?

- What is something positive about the person sitting next to you?

- What did you think about this activity?

GARDENING (CAMP 4)

Purpose of the activity

- To help participants to understand the importance of patience and impulse control

- To expose participants to new activities and hobbies to alleviate stress and tension

- To assist participants in following directions and developing responsibility

Description of the activity

The leader will discuss plants and flowers with the participants. The leader will ask the participants if plants grow quickly or slowly. The leader will discuss the order of growing a plant (pick the plant, get a container and soil, plant the seed, etc.) and if it is important to follow directions in order to have a healthy plant. The leader will then assist the group in selecting the type of plant they want to plant, and planting the plants in containers. The group members will also be allowed to decorate their plant containers.

Instructions for leaders

- The leader will begin by discussing plants and flowers with participants. He or she will ask the participants if plants grow quickly or slowly. The leader will discuss patience and impulse control during this time.

- The leader will also discuss all the steps to growing a plant and the reasons that it is important to follow directions and the correct sequence.

- The leader will then allow the participants to decorate their plant containers and select the type of plant or flower that they would like to grow.

- The participants will then get soil and plant their plants or flower.

- The leader will then discuss the ways to take care of a plant and keep it healthy.

Discussion opportunities and ideas

Listed below are questions to discuss with the participants before, during, and after the activity:

- How quickly does a plant grow?

- Why does it take time for a plant to grow?

- What happens if you try to make a plant grow faster by giving it too much water?

- Patience is an important part of growing plants and flowers. Why?

- What is the first thing you do to grow a plant?

- What would happen if you watered the plant before putting it in soil?

- Why is important to follow the steps in the correct order when gardening and planting?

- How do you take care of a plant once you have planted it?

- Whose responsibility will it be to take care of your new plant or flower?

"GREAT," "COULD-BE-BETTER," AND "UNACCEPTABLE" BEHAVIOR BEAN BAG TOSS[4] (CAMP 4)

Purpose of the activity

- To help participants identify appropriate and inappropriate ways of dealing with anger, stress, and tension

- To assist participants in developing impulse control and social skills by participating in the cooperative activity

- To promote new ways of handling stress and anger

Description of the activity

This activity is an adaptation of the traditional bean bag toss. A traditional bean bag toss involves the participants throwing bean bags through holes in a wooden board, or into buckets or bins placed at progressively greater distances away. This adaption requires three bins, one for each of the behaviors (one bin for great behaviors, one bin for could-be-better behaviors, and one bin for unacceptable behaviors). Each participant will be given ten bean bags and have ten chances to play the game. The therapist will call out a behavior and the participant will throw the bean bag into the bin that he or she believes most appropriately describes the behavior called. At the end of the activity, the participants will get to select prizes based on their number of correct responses. Participants will also be encouraged to use good social skills and manners while waiting for their turn.

Instructions for leaders

- The leader will explain to the group that they are going to participate in a bean bag toss.

- The leader will explain that he or she will be calling out behaviors and activities. The participant will decide if each one is great, could be better, or unacceptable and then attempt to toss the bean bag in the appropriate bin.

- After all participants have had a turn, the leader will then discuss the reasons that each behavior was great, could have been better, or was unacceptable with the group.

- At then end of the activity, the participants will get to select prizes based on the number of correct responses.

---

4   Adapted from an activity in Jones, A. (1998) *104 Activities that Build: Self-esteem, Teamwork, Communication, Anger Management, Self-discovery, Coping Skills.* Lusby, MD: Rec Room Publishing.

Behaviors to be called out by leaders

- Starting a fight
- Defending yourself in a fight
- Talking back to a teacher
- Swearing
- Walking away from a fight
- Taking time to cool-down
- Using drugs
- Not following directions from an adult
- Sharing with someone else
- Staying in your seat when asked
- Writing in a journal to get out your feelings
- Talking to an adult you trust about your feelings
- Keeping your hands to yourself
- Respecting yourself and others
- Taking a piece of candy without asking
- Stealing a pack of gum at the grocery store
- Rushing through your homework so you can play
- Hitting others
- Deep breathing to calm yourself down when you are angry
- Going to time out the first time you are asked
- Playing with friends who are nice to you
- Playing with friends who get you in trouble
- Treating your family with respect
- Talking when it is not your turn
- Interrupting others

- Throwing a fit when you don't get your way
- Destroying someone else's property
- Watching your brothers and sisters for your mother
- Sharing your candy with your friends
- Doing your best on your assignments
- Following directions the first time they are given
- Listening while others are talking
- Telling someone to "shut up"
- Lying to your teacher to keep a friend out of trouble
- Taking an extra juice without permission
- Playing basketball
- Watching a funny movie
- Going to school every day
- Helping your mom and dad with the chores
- Throwing your candy paper on the ground
- Leaving your toys out when your mom asked you to clean up
- Breaking someone else's toy
- Spitting on someone
- Keeping a good attitude
- Smiling
- Going for a walk to stay in shape
- Drawing a picture to calm down when you are angry
- Kicking someone on purpose
- Kicking someone by accident and not saying "I'm sorry"

- Kicking someone by accident and saying "I'm sorry"
- Being nice to the new boy in your group
- Using your inside voice when you are inside a building
- Saying "excuse me" if you bump into someone
- Chewing with your mouth closed
- Helping someone who fell down
- Eating healthy foods
- Brushing your teeth
- Taking a bath every day
- Cleaning up after yourself
- Pushing someone out of the way
- Cutting in line (pushing in)
- Helping your little brother with his homework
- Pinching someone when the teacher is not looking
- Telling someone that you hate them

- Forgetting to make your bed in the morning
- Tearing pages out of your math textbook
- Taking turns with your friends
- Telling someone you don't want to play with them unless they do what you want
- Spilling something on the floor and not cleaning it up
- Spilling something on the floor and cleaning it up
- Swearing at a teacher or adult because you are mad
- Doing what you are asked the first time you are asked
- Laughing while someone else is getting in trouble
- Starting fights between other people
- Giving someone a compliment
- Saying "thank you" and "please"

CONCRETE BLOCK/STEPPING STONE (CAMP 4)

Purpose of the activity

- To develop impulse control by participating in an art project that celebrates diversity and individuality

- To promote self-esteem and creativity by participating in the activity

- To develop social skills and positive thinking by working cooperatively with others

Description of the activity

The leader will explain to the participants that they are going to make stepping stones—see illustration. Each participant will paint and decorate a stone to reflect him- or herself, and each group will decorate one stone to represent their group. The group stones can be placed in a garden at the school or facility, if possible. The group and individual with the most creative stone will each win a prize. At the end of the camp, each group will present their stones to all the camp participants.

Instructions for leaders

- The leader will explain to the group that they are going to participate in a group and individual project that is going to give them the opportunity to get very creative and express themselves.

- The group leader will explain that they are each going to paint and decorate stepping stones to represent themselves, and that they are also going make a group stone.

- The leader will assist each participant in painting his or her stone and in developing a stone to represent the whole group.

- At the end of the camp, the group will present their stones to all the camp participants.

Discussion opportunities and ideas

Listed below are questions to discuss with your group before, during, and after the project:

- How did you come up with the idea for your personal stone?

- How did your group come up with the idea for your group stone?

- Was it easier to come up with the idea for your individual stone or the group stone?

- How did the group stone reflect each person in the group?

- How did your group work together to make the group stone?

- What did you think about the activity?

CERTIFICATE OF COMPLETION

THIS CERTIFICATE RECOGNIZES

. . . .

(NAME)

FOR SUCCESSFUL COMPLETION OF THE SUMMER CAMP PROGRAM.

CONGRATULATIONS ON A JOB WELL DONE!

WE ARE PROUD OF YOU!

PRESENTED BY . . . .

DATE. . . . .

Ideas for adapting camp activities to other settings

The activities from this camp series can easily be adapted to a group setting or day-treatment setting. The activities could be completed as three individual units or as a series of sessions focused on developing life skills. The ideal meeting time would be hourly session two to three times per week. However, the activities could be combined or conducted over a shorter period of time, based on the needs of the group. Listed below is a sample schedule for completing the activities during a one-hour group meeting twice a week.

Unit 1: Anger-control activities
WEEK 1

Session 1: Introduce the topic of anger control to the group. Complete The Color of Anger activity (p.194).

Session 2: Review anger control and The Color of Anger activity. Complete and discuss the Positive Word Wall activity (p.192).

WEEK 2

Session 1: Review and continue group discussions on anger control. Provide each member with a copy of the Animal Anger-Control Questionnaire (pp.117–118) to complete. Discuss the different animals and their anger. Discuss strategies for each animal to use when they are angry in order to help control their anger.

Session 2: Review the results from the Animal Anger-Control Questionnaire. Complete the Create a Group Totem Pole activity (p.198) based on each group member's anger style. Summarize the activities from the anger-control sessions and review appropriate anger-control strategies.

Unit 2: Impulse-control activities
WEEK 1

Session 1: Discuss impulse control with the group and ways to improve impulse control. Complete the Gardening activity (p.206) with the group. Keep each group-member's plant in the group room (if possible) and allow members to improve impulse control (patience, waiting for things to happen, providing the right amount of water) by caring for the plants over the next two weeks.

Session 2: Review impulse-control topic and activities from the previous session. Allow group members to check on their plants. Complete the "Great," "Could-Be-Better," and "Unacceptable" Behavior Bean Bag Toss with the group (p.207).

WEEK 2

Session 1: Review the impulse-control topic and activities from previous sessions. Begin the Concrete Block/Stepping Stone activity (p.210). Remind group members to show impulse control by taking their time over designing and painting the stones. Allow group members time to check on their plants.

Session 2: Review the impulse-control topic and activities. Complete the Concrete Block/Stepping Stone activity. Allow group members to take home their plants and stepping stones as visual reminders of the importance of impulse control.

Unit 3: Self-esteem activities
WEEK 1

Session 1: Introduce the self-esteem topic and ways to develop self-esteem. Begin the Kite Decorating and Flying activity (p.205) and fly kites if time allows.

Session 2: Review the self-esteem discussion and how healthy communication influences self-esteem. Complete the Silent and Verbal Water Balloon Toss activity (p.203). Substitute a regular ball if water balloons are not appropriate in your setting. Discuss the activity after completion.

WEEK 2

Session 1: Review previous discussions on self-esteem. Complete the Pull a Duck activity (p.200) and discuss.

Session 2: Self-esteem celebration. Review the discussions and activities from the past week. Serve special snacks and create a fun atmosphere to celebrate the development of self-esteem in self and other group members.

Positive-thinking and coping-skills therapeutic camp series

The colors of me

Camp 1—Green Camp/Positive Thinking
Camp 2—Red Camp/Self-Discovery
Camp 3—Blue Camp/Stress Relief and Relaxation
Camp 4—White Camp/Peacemaking and Conflict Resolution
Camp 5—Gold Camp/Reward and Closing Ceremony

There is handout that can be used to advertise the camps included on p.240. This handout can be reproduced and distributed as needed.

Purpose of the camps

The purpose of the summer therapeutic camp series is to provide children with behavioral and emotional problems an opportunity to learn new ways of behaving and to receive rewards for good behavior while participating in five fun and therapeutic camps. The theme for the camps will be "The colors of me." Each of these camps will incorporate the overall theme into the day while addressing a specific behavior or skill. Each camp will have a color of the day and a behavior or skill that is associated with that color. At the end of the day, participants who successfully completed the camp will receive a certificate that corresponds with the color of the camp. At the end of the camps, participants who have received all four Certificates of Completion (see p.241) will be eligible to participate in the reward camp.

The first four camps will be set up with rotating stations in the morning that relate to the camp's theme. The topics that will be addressed include positive thinking, self-discovery, relaxation techniques, and peacemaking. At the conclusion of each camp, participants who meet the criteria and receive a camp certificate will be able to participate in the camp's reward activity. The purpose of the rewards is to encourage children to actively participate in the camps. Reward activities include swimming, bowling, skating, and going to the movies. The final reward camp will include a trip to a local waterpark.

CAMP 1: GREEN CAMP/POSITIVE THINKING

Goals/objectives

- To assist participants in developing positive self-talk

- To help participants understand the impact of words and the importance of using positive language with others

- To help participants identify ways to self-soothe and cope with problems through the use of positive thinking

Camp itinerary

9:00—Opening session to explain the purpose of the camp (to develop positive-thinking skills). Participants will break into groups, have breakfast, and receive camp T-shirts.

9:30—Station 1: Positive Planter (p.221) to contain the Positive Words Rock Garden.

10:15—Station 2: Positive Words Rock Garden (p.223) to go in Positive Planter.

11:00—Station 3: Positive Words Beading (p.224).

11:45—Clean up and prepare for lunch.

12:00—Lunch (emphasizing social skills and functional living skills).

12:30—Clean up and receive certificates of participation.

1:00—Reward activity.

2:45—Clean up and prepare to go home.

Criteria for participating in afternoon reward

- Attend the camp

- Participate and complete each camp station

- Follow the rules and instructions given by camp leaders

- Display a good attitude and show respect for others throughout the day

Supply list

- Assorted paint colors (for planter and rocks)

- Planters (one per participant)

- Rocks (ten per participant)

- Planting soil (for rock garden)

- Decorations for planters (glitter, beads, etc.)

- ABC beads (for Positive Words Beading)

- Beads in assorted colors (for Positive Words Beading)

- Jewelry cords (for Positive Words Beading)

- Scissors (for Positive Words Beading)

- Stencils (for Positive Planters)

- Paint markers (for planter and rocks)

- Breakfast bars

- Trash bags

- Cups and plates

- Paper towels

- Hand sanitizer

- Fruit-flavored sports drink

- Icepops

- Lunch supplies

- Certificates printed on green card

CAMP 2: RED CAMP/SELF-DISCOVERY

Goals/objectives

- To assist participants in developing respect for self and others

- To help participants understand the concept of love and healthy ways to show love to self and others

- To assist participants in identifying personal likes and dislikes

Camp itinerary

9:00—Opening session to explain the purpose of the camp (to get to know ourselves). Participants will divide into groups and eat breakfast during this time.
9:30—Station 1: Bead Buddies (p.225).
10:00—Station 2: Stuffed with Love (p.226).
11:00—Station 3: Potato Sack Race (p.227).
11:20—Station 4: Taste Test (p.228).
11:45—Clean up and get ready for lunch.
12:00—Lunch (emphasizing social skills and functional living skills).
12:30—Clean up and receive certificates of participation.
1:00—Reward activity.
2:45—Clean up and get ready to go home.

Criteria for participating in afternoon reward

- Attend the camp

- Participate and complete each camp station

- Follow the rules and instructions given by camp leaders

- Display a good attitude and show respect for others throughout the day

Supply list

- Assorted colors of wood beads (for Bead Buddies)

- Assorted pipe cleaners and yarn (for Bead Buddies)

- Paint markers (for Bead Buddies and Stuffed with Love)

- Scissors or wire-cutters (for Bead Buddies)

- Newspaper (for Stuffed with Love)

- Glue (for Stuffed with Love)

- Paint (for Stuffed with Love)

- Potato sacks (for Potato Sack Race)

- Food for Taste Test (Chinese, Mexican, Italian, American)

- Breakfast bars

- Fruit-flavored sports drink

- Icepops

- Cups and plates

- Hand sanitizer

- Paper towels

- Lunch

- Certificates printed on red card

CAMP 3: BLUE CAMP/STRESS RELIEF AND RELAXATION

Goals/objectives

- To assist participants in learning healthy ways to relax and relieve stress
- To expose participants to creative ways to self-soothe and cope with problems
- To teach participants positive ways to have fun and spend leisure time

Camp itinerary

9:00—Opening session to explain the purpose of the camp (to learn new ways to relax and relieve stress). Participants will divide into groups and eat breakfast.
9:30—Station 1: Relaxation Music (p.229).
10:00—Station 2: Sand Art (p.230).
10:30—Station 3: Aromatherapy (p.231).
11:00—Station 4: Group Sand Castles (p.232).
11:45—Clean up and prepare for lunch.
12:00—Lunch (emphasizing social skills and functional living skills).
12:30—Clean up and receive certificates of participation.
1:00—Reward activity.
2:45—Clean up and get ready to go home.

Criteria for participating in afternoon reward

- Attend the camp
- Participate and complete each camp station
- Follow the rules and instructions given by camp leaders
- Display a good attitude and show respect for others throughout the day

Supply list

- Relaxation CD
- Relaxation scripts
- Play sand (for Group Sand Castles)
- Sand in assorted colors (for Sand Art)
- Bottles (for Sand Art)
- Small plastic pools (for Group Sand Castles)
- Plastic castles shapes and sand toys (for Group Sand Castles)
- Buckets and shovels (for Group Sand Castles)
- Assorted oils and scents (for Aromatherapy)
- Breakfast bars
- Fruit-flavored sports drink
- Cups and plates
- Paper towels
- Icepops
- Hand sanitizer
- Lunch
- Trash bags
- Certificates printed on blue card

CAMP 4: WHITE CAMP/PEACEMAKING AND CONFLICT RESOLUTION

Goals/objectives

- To assist children in developing healthy peacemaking and conflict-resolution skills
- To help children understand the importance of working together cooperatively and respecting individual and group differences
- To encourage children to develop good social skills

Camp itinerary

9:00—Opening session to explain the purpose of the camp (to develop peacemaking and conflict-resolution skills). Participants will divide into groups and have breakfast.
9:30—Station 1: Peacing it Together (p.234).
10:30—Station 2: Umbrella of Peace (p.236).
11:15—Station 3: Peace Sign Design (p.238).
12:00—Clean up and eat lunch.
12:30—Clean up from lunch and receive Certificates of Completion (p.241).
1:00—Reward activity.
2:45—Clean up and get ready to go home.

Criteria for participating in afternoon reward

- Attend the camp
- Participate and complete each camp station
- Follow the rules and instructions given by camp leaders
- Display a good attitude and show respect for others throughout the day

Supply list

- Newspaper (for Peacing it Together)
- Paint (for Peacing it Together)
- Tape and glue (for Peacing it Together)
- Plain white umbrellas (for Umbrellas of Peace)
- Paint (for Umbrellas of Peace)
- Stencils (for Umbrellas of Peace)
- Large piece of foam-board, cut into circles (for Peace Sign Design)
- Paint or markers (for Peace Sign Design)

- Plates and cups
- Breakfast bars
- Icepops
- Paper towels
- Lunch
- Trash bags
- Fruit-flavored sports drink
- Hand sanitizer
- Certificates printed on white card

CAMP 5: GOLD CAMP/REWARD AND CLOSING CEREMONY

Goals/objectives

- To provide a reward for participants who have successfully completed all of the summer camps

- To promote self-esteem among participants by recognizing their summer accomplishment

- To give participants an opportunity to display the behaviors and skills they have learned in a social setting

Camp itinerary

9:00—Closing ceremony. Participants will receive certificates for completion of camps.
10:15—Get ready for lunch.
10:30—Lunch.
11:30—Reward activity (local waterpark).
2:30—Clean up and get ready to go home.

Criteria for receiving certificate and attending reward camp

- Attend all camps

- Complete all camp activities and stations

- Display a positive attitude and show respect to others at all camps

- Follow the rules and comply with directions from camp leaders

Supply list

- Final Camp Certificates (see p.242, printed on colored card)

- Reward bags (with candy and small prizes)

- Breakfast bars

- Fruit-flavored sports drink

- Lunch

- Cups and plates

- Paper towels

- Trash bags

- Hand sanitizer

- Face paint

Activities

POSITIVE PLANTER (CAMP 1)

Purpose of the activity

- To help the participant develop positive-thinking skills by designing and decorating a planter with positive words and images

- To assist the participant in developing coping skills and learning to self-soothe

- To allow participant to identify positive aspects of his or her life and self

Description of the activity

Participants will create a positive planter to contain the Positive Words Rock Garden that they will also make during the camp. Suggestions for containers for the planter include wooden pencil boxes or small terracotta pots (see illustrations). The positive planter will be decorated by the participant with any positive images or phrases that he or she chooses. As part of the activity, the participant will also identify blessings and positive aspects of his or her life. The participant will be encouraged to use the planter (with the added rock garden) when he or she is discouraged or having problems, in order to shift focus to positive areas of his or her life.

Instructions for leaders

- The group leader will discuss with the participants the importance of positive versus negative thinking and assist the group in identifying positive words and thoughts.

- The group leader will assist participants in identifying things in their lives for which they are grateful.

- The group leader will explain that each participant is going to create a personal positive planter that will later be filled with the positive rock garden. The group leader will explain that participants are making these positive planters and rock gardens to remind them to think positively whenever they feel sad or discouraged.

- Each participant will be given a planter to paint and decorate with positive images.

- The group leader may assist children in identifying positive words and images.

- The participants may share their planters with the group, if desired.

Discussion opportunities and ideas

- What are some positive words, symbols, and images?

- What are some reasons it is important to think positive thoughts?

- What are some healthy ways to deal with discouragement and sadness?

- What are some positive ways you have dealt with bad things in life?

- How will you use the positive planter you are making?

- What is the difference between positive and negative thinking?

POSITIVE WORDS ROCK GARDEN (CAMP 1)

Purpose of the activity

- To assist participants in identifying positive thoughts and affirmations
- To help participants develop positive-thinking skills and self-esteem
- To encourage participants to be thankful and identify reasons to be thankful

Description of the activity

Participants will paint rocks in the colors of their choice and decorate these rocks with positive words and images of their choice. Participants will then place these rocks and potting soil or sand in the positive planter that was created in the previous activity. The participants will continue to discuss positive thinking and gratitude at this station. The group leader will remind the participants that the positive rock garden can serve as a visual reminder to think positively during difficult times.

Instructions for leaders

- The group leader will begin by discussing words, thoughts, and images that encourage us and make us feel better when we are having a bad day.
- The leader will tell the group that they are going to create positive rock gardens to place in their positive planters and use when they feel sad or discouraged.
- The leader will pass out rocks to each participants and allow time to paint and decorate the rocks.
- After the rocks have been painted, the leader will assist participants in identifying positive words or phrases to put on their rocks.
- Once the words have been written on the rocks and they have dried, the participants will put them in their planters to create a positive rock garden.
- The participants will be given the opportunity to share their planters with the group.

Discussion opportunities and ideas

- What are some words and thoughts that make you feel better when you are having a bad day?
- What are some words and thoughts that help you calm down when you are angry?
- How do the words we say and think impact on us?
- How do you feel when others say something nice to you? What about something horrible?
- What are some positive ways to deal with sadness?
- How will you use your positive rock garden?

POSITIVE WORDS BEADING (CAMP 1)

Purpose of the activity

- To continue to reinforce the importance of positive thinking

- To encourage participants to choose their thoughts and words carefully

- To assist participants in understanding the importance of our words

Description of the activity

The leader will discuss the power of words with the participants and help participants identify times when words have helped or hurt them in the past. The leader will also help participants identify reasons why it is important to choose our thoughts and word carefully. The participants will have the opportunity to make positive words jewelry (bracelets, necklaces, etc.) using alphabet and colored beads.

Instructions for leaders

- The leader will ask participants to give examples of the power of words and thoughts as well as times that words have helped or hurt them.

- The leader will use these examples to discuss the reasons it is important to choose our words carefully.

- The group members will then have an opportunity to make "positive" necklaces, bracelets and other jewelry using alphabet plastic beads, colored plastic beads, and jewelry cord.

- The participants will use the alphabet beads to spell out words and phrases that are positive and encouraging to them.

Discussion opportunities and ideas

- Tell us about a time you used words to help someone.

- What are some ways we use words to hurt others? What can we do differently?

- Why do we need to choose our words carefully?

- How can you use words to encourage others?

- How can you use words to encourage yourself?

- How will you use your positive jewelry?

BEAD BUDDIES (CAMP 2)

Purpose of the activity

- To assist participants in developing respect for self and others
- To encourage self-esteem and social skills
- To identify ways to treat self and others with respect

Description of the activity

Each participant will create two Bead Buddies to represent him- or herself and a friend who treats him or her with respect. The leader will discuss respect and self-esteem with the group, and assist each participant in identifying ways to treat others with respect and develop healthy self-esteem.

Instructions for leaders

- The leader will begin by discussing ways to treat ourselves and others with respect.
- The leader will assist the group in understanding what respect is and why it is important to treat others respectfully.
- The leader will explain to the group that they are going to create Bead Buddies to represent themselves and their best friend.
- The leader will explain that the purpose of the Bead Buddies is to remind the participants to treat themselves and their friends with respect.
- Bead Buddies are made by twisting two pipe cleaners together to form an X. These are the arms and legs. A third pipe cleaner is cut in half and twisted around the center of the X, pointing up to serve as the head. Beads are then added to each end of the pipe cleaner.

Discussion opportunities and ideas

- What is respect?
- How can you show respect for yourself and others?
- Describe a friend who treats you with respect.
- What are some ways to show respect to adults?
- What does respect have to do with how you feel about yourself?
- How will you use your Bead Buddies?

STUFFED WITH LOVE (CAMP 2)

Purpose of the activity

- To assist participants in gaining understanding of love and the different types of love
- To help participants identify appropriate and healthy ways to show love for family and friends
- To develop social skills and self-esteem by working cooperatively as a group

Description of the activity

The participants will work together to create a heart made out of newspaper. As the group is constructing the heart, the leader will discuss love with the group, healthy ways to show love, and different types of love.

Instructions for leaders

- Divide participants in groups of two or three. Give each group two large hearts cut out of newspaper and paint. Give the group time to paint and decorate their hearts.
- When complete, set the hearts aside to dry.
- While hearts are drying, lead a group discussion about love. Assist the group in defining love and helping the group members identify healthy ways to show love to others.
- When the hearts are dry, staple them together around the bottom with the painted sides of the heart facing outward. Leave a hole at the top. Allow group members to stuff the hole with leftover newspaper. Finish stapling the heart until it is completely shut.
- Provide an opportunity for group members to share their Stuffed with Love hearts with the group.

Discussion opportunities and ideas

- What is love?
- How do we show love to our family?
- How do we show love to our friends?
- How do we show love to ourselves?
- How did you show love to the other group members when you were working together to create the Stuffed with Love hearts?
- What do our Stuffed with Love hearts represent?

POTATO SACK RACE (CAMP 2)

Purpose of the activity

- To develop social skills/self-esteem
- To exhibit good sportsmanship before, during, and after the activity
- To show respect for other participants and adults

Description of the activity

The group members will participate in a traditional sack race in small groups of eight to ten participants. The winner of each small group race will participate in a championship sack race at the end of the camp. Small prizes will be available for the winners. The group leader will discuss the importance of showing respect for others and exhibiting good sportsmanship during the activity. In addition to the winner, the group leader will select one participant from each group who exhibited good sportsmanship throughout the activity to receive a prize.

Instructions for leaders

- The group leader will review the importance of showing respect for others and assist the group in identifying ways to show good sportsmanship.

- The group will participate in a traditional sack race to give the group members an opportunity to display these skills in a real situation.

- After the activity is complete, the group leader will debrief the group by identifying ways that each member exhibited good sportsmanship. The group leader will select one member who exhibited very good sportsmanship to receive a small prize. All members will receive a special snack (such as icepops or chips) for participating at the end of the camp.

- The winner of the sack race from each group will participate in a championship race at the end of the camp to give participants another opportunity to show good sportsmanship and display respect for others.

Discussion opportunities and ideas

- What are some ways to show respect for others when we are playing sports or competing against one another?
- What is good sportsmanship?
- What are some ways to show good sportsmanship when you lose?
- What are some ways to show good sportsmanship when you win?
- How can we avoid being "sore losers"?

TASTE TEST (CAMP 2)

Purpose of the activity

- To expose participants to new things and help them identify their likes and dislikes

- To develop functional living skills by exhibiting good table manners

- To improve self-esteem and social skills by trying something new

Description of the activity

Participants will be given the opportunity to taste a variety of different foods such as Chinese, Mexican, Italian, and American. These samples will be purchased at local restaurants. The participants will have the opportunity to rate the foods they like and do not like. The group leader will use the opportunity to discuss trying new things and being open to possibilities with the group. The group leader will discuss individual differences with the group by explaining that each member has different likes and dislikes.

Instructions for leaders

- The group leader will begin by explaining that the participants are going to have a taste test and to sample foods that they may have never tried before. The leader will explain that each group member can decide which foods he or she likes or dislikes. At the end of the activity, the participants will share their likes and dislikes with each other.

- The leader will discuss the importance of being open to trying new things and being open-minded even when things may not "look" good.

- After the group members have tasted all the foods and shared their likes and dislikes with each other, the leader will discuss individual differences with the group.

- The leader will explain to the group that each person is unique and special. Not everyone has the same favorite food or does things the same way, but the world is more interesting because each person is different.

Discussion opportunities and ideas

- What are some reasons to try new things?

- What are some reasons not to try new things?

- What might happen if you do not ever try anything new or different?

- What can you do if you are afraid to try something new?

- When we talked about our favorite foods, did everyone choose the same one? Why not?

- What would the world be like if we were all the same?

- How can we treat others who are different from us with respect?

RELAXATION MUSIC (CAMP 3)

(See Chapter 4, p.108, for "Relaxing music checklist".)

Purpose of the activity

- To learn new ways to relax and self-soothe
- To identify a healthy way to relieve anger and stress
- To assist participants in understanding the importance of relaxation

Description of the activity

The leader will begin by explaining to the group that they are going to learn a new way to relax. The leader will ask the group member to find a comfortable spot. The leader will give each participant a pencil and a checklist with a listing of different types of music. The leader will play short samples of different types of music and ask the participants to put a checkmark by the types of music that relax and calm them. (Depending on the number of participants, CDs could be created of the relaxation music chosen by each participant.)

Instructions for leaders

- The leader will begin by discussing with the group relaxation and reasons why it is important to relax.
- After the initial discussion, the leader will ask group members to find a comfortable spot and distribute checklists and pencils.
- The leader will play a short sample of different music genres for the group to listen to and decide which music is relaxing.
- The leader will ask the group members to put a mark by the music that is relaxing to them.
- After all the music has been played, the group will discuss the different types of music and which types were most relaxing to them.
- If possible, CDs may be created of the music chosen by the group members.

Discussion opportunities and ideas

- What does it mean to relax?
- Why is it important to know how to relax?
- What are some different ways to relax?
- How can you use relaxation techniques to calm yourself when you are angry or upset?
- How did you feel when the music was playing?
- What did your body do when listening to relaxing music?
- What can you take away from this activity to help you relax in the future?
- What did you like about this activity?

SAND ART (CAMP 3)

Purpose of the activity

- To assist participants in identifying positive ways to relax and enjoy leisure time

- To encourage social skills and self-esteem by participating in a cooperative setting

- To expose participants to a variety of relaxation techniques and methods of self-soothing

Description of the activity

The leader will begin by explaining to the participants that there are many different ways to relax and calm down when they are upset or stressed. The group will identify some of the ways (such as listen to music, take a walk, write in a journal, etc.). The leader will explain that some people relax through art activities. The leader will explain to the group that they are going to create sand art in bottles to take home with them as a reminder to relax. The participants will all have an opportunity to decorate a bottle and fill it with different colored sands of their choosing.

Instructions for leaders

- The leader will discuss with the group the many different ways there are to relax and assist the group in identifying some of the ways they have learned to relax at the camp.

- The leader will also explain to the group that some people relax through creating art. This activity will give the group members an opportunity to experience this process.

- The leader will explain to the group that they will be able to take home their sand art bottles as reminder of the importance of relaxation.

- The leader will allow each participant to select a bottle for the sand art and distribute materials (colored sand and funnels) to each table.

- Group members will create their sand art by choosing different colored sand to add to their bottles.

- At the end of the activity, the leader will discuss the experience with the group.

- The participants may present their bottles to the group if desired.

Discussion opportunities and ideas

- What are some of the ways that you have learned to relax today?

- Does everyone choose to relax in the same way?

- Why is it important to know how to relax?

- What does it mean to be stressed?

- What does this sand art you are creating represent? How can you use it at home?

- What did you like about this activity?

AROMATHERAPY (CAMP 3)

(See Chapter 4, p.108, for "Aromatherapy checklist".)

Purpose of the activity

- To assist participants in identifying different ways to relax and relieve stress
- To expose participants to new experiences
- To promote wellness and self-esteem among participants

Description of the activity

The leader will begin by discussing some of the different ways to relax with the group (including the ones they have participated in during the camp). The leader will explain that another way to relax is to use our senses. The leader will tell the group that during this activity the group members are going to use their sense of smell to relax. Each participant will have an opportunity to smell different oils and scents and identify the ones that are soothing and relaxing to him or her. If possible, participants could be provided with small samples of the scents that they found relaxing to take home with them.

Instructions for leaders

- The leader will discuss with the group all the different methods of relaxation that they are have learned and participated in during the camp.
- The leader will explain that during this activity they are going to learn a new way to relax using their senses. The leader will discuss the different senses with the group and some of the ways to use our senses to relax.
- The leader will have a table set up with several different oils and scents for the participants to smell. Each participant will be given a checklist and pencil to mark the scents that he or she finds relaxing.
- After all the participants have had a chance to smell the scents and oils, the leader will discuss the activity with the group and how they felt while participating in the activity.
- If possible, provide small samples of the relaxing scents for the participants to take home.

Discussion opportunities and ideas

- What are some ways you have learned to relax today?
- Which one did you like the best so far?
- How can we use our senses to relax?
- What are some different ways to use our senses (sense of sight, sense of smell, sense of touch) to calm down?
- Which smells did you like the best during this activity?
- Did any of the scents help you feel more relaxed?
- What can you take away from the activity to help you relax when you are alone?

GROUP SAND CASTLES (CAMP 3)

Purpose of the activity

- To identify ways to relax and have fun as a group
- To promote good social skills and to learn to work cooperatively as a group
- To experience new ways to relax

Description of the activity

The leader will review all the relaxation methods the participants have learned during the camp. The leader will also discuss ways to relax and enjoy leisure time in a group. Each group will work together to make a sand castle. Each group will have a plastic pool, play sand, sand molds, sand toys and water buckets. After completing the activity, the leader will discuss the experience with the group. At the end of the camp, the group will present their sand castles to all the participants.

Instructions for leaders

- The leader will review all of the relaxation methods the participants have learned throughout the camp. The participants will discuss which activities they liked best.
- The leader will explain that they are going to create a group sand castle and learn to relax and have fun as a group.
- Each group (four to six participants in a group) will have a station set up with a plastic pool, sand, water buckets, and sand molds to create their sand castle.
- The group leader will tell the groups that the only rule is to treat other group members with respect. The groups will decide how to create their sand castles.

- The group leader will observe the interactions between group members.
- After the sand castles are completed, the leader will discuss the activity with the group as well as how each group worked as a team.
- At the end of the camp, the groups will have the opportunity to present their sand castle to the other camp participants.

Discussion opportunities and ideas

- What are some ways you have learned to relax today?
- Which relaxation activity did you like the best? Why?
- How can you use these activities at home?
- What did you like about this activity?
- Were you able to relax and have fun while working with a group?
- What was it like working with your group to make a sand castle?
- Can you relax and have fun at the same time?
- What is one thing you can do in the future when you are feeling stressed out or upset?

PEACING IT TOGETHER (CAMP 4)

Purpose of the activity

- To learn healthy conflict-resolution skills

- To cooperate as a group and develop positive social skills

- To promote awareness of ways to interact peacefully with others

Description of the activity

The camp participants will together make a "peace" animal (ideas include a fish, a bird, a dog, a giraffe, or a monkey, depending on the number of groups of participants and number of body parts needed). Each group will make one part of the "peace" animal. For example, if making a dog, one group would make a leg, one group would make the tail, one group would make the head, etc. The participants will make their part by cutting newspaper or large paper to the size needed for the body part, painting the pieces for the body part, stapling or gluing together the part, and then stuffing it with tissue paper or newspaper before completely closing it up. For example, if making the tail of the dog, two long strips of equal length paper would be cut and painted.

Once dry, it would be stapled together around the bottom portion, stuffed with paper scraps, and then completely shut. At the end of the camp, by using duct tape or masking tape with the help of other needed supports (boxes and stones to hold it up), all of the parts of the animal would be "peaced" together to create an animal that represents all of the camp participants.

Instructions for leaders

- The leader will begin by discussing ways to work together and live peacefully. The group will identify examples of, and reasons for, living peacefully and respecting individual differences.

- The leader will explain to the group that the camp participants are going to construct a peace animal. Each group will be assigned a different part of the animal to create.

- The group will be given the needed materials (large paper, scissors, paint, brushes, stapler, glue, or masking tape) to create their part.

- The leader will provide assistance as needed.

- After the body part is complete, the leader will discuss the experience with the group and help them identify ways that they worked together peacefully.

- At the conclusion of the camp, groups will put their parts together to create a camp peace animal.

Discussion opportunities and ideas

- What is peace?
- What does it mean to live peacefully with other people?
- How can we have peace with people who are different from us, or people we do not like?
- What would the world be like if everyone were just the same?
- How can you show peace to other people?
- What are some ways to work with others in a peaceful manner?
- What does the peace animal represent?
- Why is each group only making one part of the animal?
- What is one thing you can do at home to promote peace in your family?
- What did you think about this activity?

UMBRELLA OF PEACE[5] (CAMP 4)

Purpose of the activity

- To help participants identify ways to resolve problems and encourage positive interaction

- To help participants learn to get along with others in a peaceful manner

- To promote self-esteem and social skills among participants

Description of the activity

The participants will create an umbrella of peace to help them remember the concepts they have learned during the camp. The leader will discuss peaceful thoughts, ways to peacefully resolve conflict, ways to encourage peace in others, and ways to protect themselves when conflict occurs. The participants will decorate and paint a white umbrella with peaceful symbols and images—see illustrations. Participants will take these umbrellas home as a visual reminder to live peacefully, even when conflict occurs.

Instructions for leaders

- The leader will discuss peace with the group, including what peace is, how to promote and encourage peace with others, how to peacefully resolve conflict, and how to protect oneself when conflict gets out of control.

- The leader will help the group members identify examples of peaceful thoughts and images, as well as examples of when they have resolved conflict peacefully in the past.

---

5   Adapted from an activity first learned about in a presentation by Dr. Joe Ray Underwood and Nancy Underwood at the Mississippi Counseling Association Annual Conference 2007.

- The leader will distribute supplies (one umbrella per participant, stencils, waterproof paint, brushes).

- Each participant will have the opportunity to create his or her personal umbrella of peace to serve as a reminder to live peacefully when the camp is over.

- The participants will have the opportunity to share their umbrellas with the group and talk about what the symbols on their umbrellas represent.

Discussion opportunities and ideas

- What are some peaceful thoughts?

- What are some peaceful ways to resolve a conflict?

- Tell us about a time you peacefully resolved conflict in the past.

- How can you encourage peace at home? At school? With your friends?

- What are some symbols that represent peace?

- Why is peace important?

- What are some peaceful words or images that you can put on your umbrella?

PEACE SIGN DESIGN[6] (CAMP 4)

Purpose of the activity

- To identify what peace means to each participant and group

- To encourage social skills and cooperation by working together on a group activity

- To understand the importance of promoting peace with others

Description of the activity

Each group will be given a large piece of foam-board (although this could also be made out of plywood for durability) with the outline of a peace sign drawn on it (see illustrations). The leader will explain that the group is going to work together to define what peace means to each of them by drawing and writing phrases (using markers or paint) on the peace sign. The group will consider what peace means in different areas of life including home, school, with friends, etc. At the end of the camp, each group will present their peace sign to the other camp participants.

Instructions for leaders

- The leader will ask each group member to spend a few minutes quietly thinking about what peace means to him or her. The leader will encourage them to think about all the different parts of his or her life and how peace applies to each part.

- The leader will show each group the large peace sign and explain that each group is going to work together to determine what to write and draw on their peace sign.

---

6   Adapted from an activity first learned about in a presentation by Dr. Joe Ray Underwood and Nancy Underwood at the Mississippi Counseling Association Annual Conference 2007.

- The leader will distribute materials (peace signs, markers or paint) and assist groups as needed.

- All group members should be included and have an opportunity to add to the peace sign.

- After the peace sign is complete, the group will discuss the process of making the peace sign.

- At the conclusion of the camp, the group members will have the opportunity to present their peace sign to all the camp participants.

Discussion opportunities and ideas

- What does peace mean to you in each area of your life?

- How can you work together on this peace sign and include everyone in your group?

- How did you decide which images and symbols to include on your peace sign?

- What was it like working with your group on the peace sign?

- Did everyone have the same idea for the peace sign? How did you resolve this?

- What is one way you can promote peace in your life?

- What have you learned about peace today?

- What did you think about this activity?

Summer Camp for Kids!

Camps meeting in . . . .
(MONTH/S)

from . . . .
(START AND END TIME)

We are looking forward to your child participating in this character education program!

Get ready for lots of fun, including:
Arts and Crafts, Social Skills Activities, Special Snacks, Games and Prizes, Outdoor Activities, Goal Setting, Self-Esteem Enhancement, Reward Field Trips, in a positive and therapeutic environment.

Lunch, snacks, and transportation are provided.

Participants will be given T-shirts to wear.

Reward trips are planned for participants with good behavior!

For more information, contact us at . . . .
(PHONE NUMBER)

CERTIFICATE OF COMPLETION

THIS CERTIFICATE RECOGNIZES

. . . .

(NAME)

FOR COMPLETING

. . . .

(COLOR/NAME OF CAMP)

PRESENTED BY . . . .

DATE . . . .

✓

CERTIFICATE OF COMPLETION

THIS CERTIFICATE RECOGNIZES

. . . .

(NAME)

FOR SUCCESSFUL COMPLETION OF ALL CAMPS IN
THE SUMMER CAMP SERIES.

WE ARE PROUD OF YOU!

PRESENTED BY . . . .

DATE. . . . .

Ideas for adapting camp activities to other settings

Many of the activities in these camps can easily be adapted to a group setting. The camp activities can be adapted as four independent units or themes, or as a four-unit character-education series concluding with a ceremony and celebration for completion. Participants may earn a certificate for each unit completed. Participants earning all four certificates will be able to participate in the ceremony and celebration. The certificate system can be modified to work for your groups. For example, adjustments could be made for participants who begin attending group in the middle of the unit or miss sessions due to extenuating circumstances.

Listed below is a sample schedule for a group that meets three times per week for one hour. The schedule could easily be extended or condensed, depending on the needs of your group. For more details and instructions for each activity, see the descriptions in the camp section.

Week 1: Green/Positive Thinking

SESSION 1

Discuss positive thinking as a group. Identify examples of positive thinking and ways to develop these skills. Begin the Positive Planter activity (p.221).

SESSION 2

Review the previous discussion on positive thinking. Complete the Positive Planter activity and Positive Word Rocks. If time allows, combine to create Positive Words Rock Garden (p.223).

SESSION 3

Review the previous discussions on positive thinking. If needed, complete the Positive Words Rock Garden activity. Complete the Positive Words Beading activity (p.224). Present group members who have participated in all activities and discussions with a Certificate of Completion (see the certificate on p.241) which has been printed on green paper.

Week 2: Red/Self-Discovery

SESSION 1

Introduction of self-discovery topic to the group. Complete the Bead Buddies activity (p.225).

SESSION 2

Review the previous discussion on self-discovery with the group. Complete the Stuffed with Love activity (p.226). Display in the group room if possible.

SESSION 3

Review the previous discussion on self-discovery. Complete the Taste Test activity (p.228) and the Potato Sack Race activity (p.227). Present group members who have participated in all activities and discussions with a Certificate of Completion printed on red paper.

Week 3: Blue/Stress Relief and Relaxation

SESSION 1

Introduce the topic to the group by discussing stress management, relaxation techniques, and leisure time. Complete the Relaxation Music activity (p.229) and the Aromatherapy activity (p.231).

SESSION 2

Review the previous discussion on relaxation. Complete the Sand Art activity (p.230).

SESSION 3

Review the previous discussion on relaxation. Complete the Group Sand Castles activity (p.232—in an outdoor space). Present group members who have participated in all activities with a Certificate of Completion printed on blue paper.

Week 4: White/Peacemaking and Conflict Resolution

SESSION 1

Introduce the topic to the group by discussing peaceful ways to resolve conflict and act as peacemakers. Complete the Peace Sign Design activity (p.238).

SESSION 2

Review the previous discussion on peacemaking and conflict resolution. Begin the Umbrella of Peace activity (p.236).

SESSION 3

Review the previous discussion on peacemaking and conflict resolution. Complete the Umbrella of Peace activity (p.236).

Week 5: Continue White/Peacemaking and Conflict Resolution, and go on to Gold/Ceremonies

SESSION 1

Review the discussion from sessions on peacing it toge and conflict resolution. Begin the Peacing it Together activity (p.234).

SESSION 2

Review and complete the Peacing it Together activity by assembling the individual parts together. Present each group member who has participated in the discussions and activities with a Certificate of Completion printed on white paper.

SESSION 3

Gold Day/Ceremony and Reward. Have a ceremony to recognize participants who have completed all four units and earned certificates for all four units. Present them with a Certificate of Completion printed on gold paper. After the ceremony, have a fun day with special snacks, music, and games to celebrate the completion of these four units.

Ideas for therapeutic day programs

Many day-treatment programs and other therapeutic programs last for several hours, with one therapist or counselor leading the group throughout the time. This format puts a heavy burden on the counselor to develop therapeutic and interesting activities to use throughout the time the group meets each day. In addition, most counselors have a preferred format of counseling that may not work well with all of their clients. A rotation schedule can solve this problem. If there are several day programs that can rotate between therapists, this format works well. However, individual counselors can also use this format for their group to reach clients with different learning styles and multiple intelligences. It can also be used for programs that meet daily for short periods of time (using a different rotation each day) or weekly (using a different rotation each week).

Sample Rotation Schedule

THERAPEUTIC TOPIC FOR THE WEEK: SOCIAL SKILLS DEVELOPMENT

> Counselor 1: Art and crafts activities relating to social skills development
> Counselor 2: Role-playing activities relating to social skills development
> Counselor 3: Interactive games relating to social skills development
> Counselor 4: Bibliotherapy and group discussion relating to social skills development
> Counselor 5: Music and journaling relating to social skills development
> Counselor 6: Recreation activities relating to social skills development

DAILY SCHEDULE (EACH GROUP WILL BEGIN WITH A DIFFERENT ROTATION)

> 9:00—Program begins. Check-in with primary group leader and prepare for the day.
> 9:30—Rotation 1 (Arts and crafts).
> 10:00—Change groups.
> 10:05—Rotation 2 (Role-playing).
> 10:35—Change groups.
> 10:40—Rotation 3 (Interactive games).
> 11:10   Change groups.
> 11:15—Rotation 4 (Bibliotherapy and lunch).
> 12:15—Change groups.
> 12:20—Rotation 5 (Music and journaling).
> 12:50—Change groups.
> 12:55—Rotation 6 (Recreation).
> 1:25—Change groups.
> 1:30—Return to primary group leader, snack, and prepare to end the group for the day.

There are several advantages to this schedule. First, participants enjoy it because there is variety and movement built into each day. The behavior of participants also seems to improve based on the increased enjoyment of the program. In addition, counselors only have to plan for one lesson each day (each counselor is responsible for one rotation), which leads to higher quality therapeutic activities and less counselor burnout. Finally, participants are presented with therapeutic lessons in several different formats, increasing the chances of learning and retention of the information. Each week, there will be a different therapeutic skill to focus on during the rotations. Examples include: communication, conflict-resolution skills, anger control, and functional living skills.

In order for the rotation schedule to work, a consistent behavior plan to be used by all counselors involved is needed. A sample weekly behavior card is shown over the page, and information on how to use it is given below.

Information about the Rotation Behavior Plan

- Print the weekly behavior card on card to help with durability.

- If each group has a second staff member, have them escort the group to the next counselor and give the behavior cards to the counselor. If not, designate a trustworthy group member to deliver the cards.

- Be sure to include behavior during transitions from group to group into the behavior plan. The transitions can either be designated to be included with the behavior for the previous rotation or included in a category just for transitions.

- Based on established program rules, each participant will either receive a "yes" during the rotation for acceptable behavior or a "no" for unacceptable behavior.

- The counselor will either circle "yes" or "no" and then initial beside the choice to reduce the possibility of participants changing the selection.

- The listing for Rotation 7 is for the primary group leader to evaluate behavior while the child is with him or her at the beginning and end of the day.

- At then end of the day, the primary group leader will total the number of "yes" selections and "no" selections. If the participant received at least four "yes" selections, he or she will receive a small prize or access to a preferred privilege. (If desired, the qualifications for receiving rewards can be made more stringent.)

- At the end of the week, participants will receive levels of rewards or privileges based on the number of "yes" selections received during the week. Based on your program and the functioning level of the participants, you can determine how many "yes" selections are needed for each level.

- Be sure to include a variety of reward options and privileges at each level to reduce boredom and keep the children interested in earning prizes.

- Send parents a copy of the behavior card each day and place a copy of the weekly card in each participant's file to track progress.

- The sample weekly behavior card shown includes cards for three participants, which can be cut apart if desired.

Rotation Behavior Plan

Child's Name					Week of					
	Monday		Tuesday		Wednesday		Thursday		Friday	
Station 1	Yes	No	Yes	No	Yes	No	Yes	No	Yes	No
Station 2	Yes	No	Yes	No	Yes	No	Yes	No	Yes	No
Station 3	Yes	No	Yes	No	Yes	No	Yes	No	Yes	No
Station 4	Yes	No	Yes	No	Yes	No	Yes	No	Yes	No
Station 5	Yes	No	Yes	No	Yes	No	Yes	No	Yes	No
Station 6	Yes	No	Yes	No	Yes	No	Yes	No	Yes	No
Station 7 (Leader)	Yes	No	Yes	No	Yes	No	Yes	No	Yes	No
Total										

Child's Name					Week of					
	Monday		Tuesday		Wednesday		Thursday		Friday	
Station 1	Yes	No	Yes	No	Yes	No	Yes	No	Yes	No
Station 2	Yes	No	Yes	No	Yes	No	Yes	No	Yes	No
Station 3	Yes	No	Yes	No	Yes	No	Yes	No	Yes	No
Station 4	Yes	No	Yes	No	Yes	No	Yes	No	Yes	No
Station 5	Yes	No	Yes	No	Yes	No	Yes	No	Yes	No
Station 6	Yes	No	Yes	No	Yes	No	Yes	No	Yes	No
Station 7 (Leader)	Yes	No	Yes	No	Yes	No	Yes	No	Yes	No
Total										

Child's Name					Week of					
	Monday		Tuesday		Wednesday		Thursday		Friday	
Station 1	Yes	No	Yes	No	Yes	No	Yes	No	Yes	No
Station 2	Yes	No	Yes	No	Yes	No	Yes	No	Yes	No
Station 3	Yes	No	Yes	No	Yes	No	Yes	No	Yes	No
Station 4	Yes	No	Yes	No	Yes	No	Yes	No	Yes	No
Station 5	Yes	No	Yes	No	Yes	No	Yes	No	Yes	No
Station 6	Yes	No	Yes	No	Yes	No	Yes	No	Yes	No
Station 7 (Leader)	Yes	No	Yes	No	Yes	No	Yes	No	Yes	No
Total										

Resources

For art and craft supplies

Oriental Trading Company: www.orientaltrading.com

S & S Worldwide: www.ssww.com

Dick Blick Art Supplies: www.dickblick.com

For copies of books and movies listed in Chapter 2

Amazon (United States): www.amazon.com

Amazon (Canada): www.amazon.ca

Amazon (United Kingdom): www.amazon.co.uk

Angus & Robertson (Australia): www.angusrobertson.com.au

Barnes & Noble (United States): www.barnesandnoble.com

Books-A-Million (United States): www.booksamillion.com

Chapters Indigo (Canada): www.chapters.indigo.ca

Dymocks (Australia): www.dymocks.com.au

Play.com (United Kingdom and Europe): www.play.com

Waterstone's (United Kingdom): www.waterstones.com

WHSmith (United Kingdom): www.whsmith.co.uk

For further information on specific activities

It's a Dog's Life (Chapter 1): www.nationalkennelclub.com

Quote Quests (Chapter 3): www.brainyquote.com

Dr. Martin Luther King, Jr.'s Birthday (Chapter 4): www.thekingcenter.org/drmlkingjr; www.whitehouse.gov/about/presidents/barackobama

Rhythm and Blues (Chapter 4): www.blues.org; www.msbluestrail.org; www.longriver.net/hunt.html

For further information on specific holidays/events

MLK Jr. Holiday: www.thekingcenter.org/KingHoliday/Default.aspx

Black History Month: www.blackhistory.com

Children's Mental Health Week: www.ffcmh.org

Grandparents' Day: www.grandparents-day.com

Tailgate Party: http://en.wikipedia.org/wiki/Tailgate_party

Thanksgiving Day: http://en.wikipedia.org/wiki/Thanksgiving

Index of Purposes of Activities

Purpose	Activity	Page number
African-Americans, identifying character traits in famous	Black History Program	105
anger management	UP Day, DOWN Day Journals	28
	Bead Meaning Bracelets	82
	What's Bugging Me	85
	Anger-Control Totem Poles	116
	Positive Word Wall	192
	The Color of Anger	194
	Animal Anger-Control Questionnaire	196
	Create a Group Totem Pole	198
	"Great," "Could-Be-Better," and "Unacceptable" Behavior Bean Bag Toss	207
	Relaxation Music	229
bad behavior, identifying reasons for	Scaring Away Bad Behavior	139
calming down and self-soothing	Take a (Spring) Break and Relax	107
	The Color of Anger	194
choices, learning to make careful	The Butterfly Story	162
Christmas, appreciating joys of	Polar Express	145
communication skills	"Beanie Baby" Beginnings	34
	Pull a Duck	200
	Carousel Ride and Face Painting	202
	Silent and Verbal Water Balloon Toss	203
conflict-resolution skills	The True Story of the Three Little Pigs	52
	Enemy Pie	57
	What's Bugging Me	85
	Animal Anger-Control Questionnaire	196
	Create a Group Totem Pole	198
	Peacing it Together	234
cooperation	Creative Cookbook	84
	Pot of Gold Scavenger Hunt	106
	Giving Back Baskets	142
	Group Cheers/Chants	157
	Positive Parachute	160
	Sand Art	230
	Group Sand Castles	232
	Umbrella of Peace	236
	Peace Sign Design	238

coping skills	Art Journals	27
	UP Day, DOWN Day Journals	28
	Journal Jams	30
	Covered with Love Journals	31
	Stories and Snacks	33
	Soul Shine Sunshine	81
	Bead Meaning Bracelets	82
	What's Bugging Me	85
	Rhythm and Blues	104
	Take a (Spring) Break and Relax	107
	Growing a Garden of Mental Health	110
	Sand Art	128
	Thankful Turkey	140
	Sticks and Stones	164
	Positive Planter	221
creative thought process and creativity	Picture Prompts	18
	What's the Story?	24
	Art Journals	27
	Journal Jars	29
	Color Coding	74
	Soul Shine Sunshine	81
	Zoo Crew/Jungle People	83
	Creative Cookbook	84
	Chinese Dragons	90
	Stuffed with Love	100
	Candy Cards	102
	April Showers Bring May Flowers	109
	Group Sand Castles	127
	Sand Art	128
	Painted Pumpkins	138
	Positive Parachute	160
	Carousel Ride and Face Painting	202
	Kite Decorating and Flying	205
	Concrete Block/Stepping Stone	210
critical thinking skills	What's the Story?	24
	Journal Jars	29
decision making	*The Wizard of Oz*	40
	The Butterfly Story	162
depressed adolescents, involving	Picture Prompts	18
diary, creating a personal	Covered with Love Journals	31
diversity	Black History Program	105
dreams, expressing	*A Raisin in the Sun*	43
empathy	*Purplicious*	54
	Peaceful Earth	110
	Step by Step	113
	Giving Back Baskets	142
enjoying oneself	*Alexander and the Terrible, Horrible, No Good, Very Bad Day*	49
families, identifying types of	Family Tree	134

family history, learning about	Family Tree	134
family roles and relationships	*A Raisin in the Sun*	43
feelings, expressing	UP Day, DOWN Day Journals	28
	Journal Jams	30
	Covered with Love Journals	31
	"Beanie Baby" Beginnings	34
	Color Coding	74
following directions	Pot of Gold Scavenger Hunt	106
	Tailgate Party	132
	Gardening	206
friend, identify qualities of a good	*Purplicious*	54
	Enemy Pie	57
generosity	*Rainbow Fish*	60
	Mosaic Mascots	69
	Bead Buddies	115
	Giving Back Baskets	142
getting to know each other	What's the Story?	24
	Spirit Banner	156
goal setting	*Legally Blonde*	38
	Dream/Goal Boards	75
	Chinese Dragons	90
	Banking on Goal Setting	158
goals, achieving	Recipe for Success/"When Dreams Come True" Day	95
	Preliminary Goal Setting	155
	Goal Progress Check	159
	Poster Goal Commitment	161
	Action Steps Windsocks	168
goals vs. dreams	Dream/Goal Boards	75
good behavior	Tailgate Party	132
good things resulting from bad events	Timeline	65
grandparents, appreciating	Family Tree	134
gratitude, showing	Gratitude Journals	26
	Positive Words Rock Garden	223
greedy, not being	*Rainbow Fish*	60
group discussion	Quote Quests	72
group unity	Sign In and Begin	32
	Zoo Crew/Jungle People	83
	Group Cheers/Chants	157
	Create a Group Totem Pole	198
historical figures, importance of	Recipe for Success/"When Dreams Come True" Day	95
hope and future possibilities	City of Hope	67
hurtful words, releasing	*The Blind Side*	36
introductions	It's a Dog's Life	22
kindness	*Mean Girls*	45
	Sticks and Stones	164
leisure activities	Group Sand Castles	127
	Sand Art	230
life events, identifying, processing and reframing	Timeline	65
	Dear Younger Self	77

life skills	Creative Cookbook	84
	Safety Spiders	136
love	Stuffed with Love	100
	Candy Cards	102
	Stuffed with Love	226
mental health and wellness	Growing a Garden of Mental Health	111
mentoring	Dear Younger Self	77
morals	If	47
nature appreciation	Peaceful Earth	110
negativity, releasing	The Blind Side	36
	Alexander and the Terrible, Horrible, No Good, Very Bad Day	49
	Knocking Down Negativity	71
	Positive/Negative Word Walls	80
	Rhythm and Blues	104
	Dream Catchers	167
obstacles, overcoming	Legally Blonde	38
opposition, handling	"I Have a Dream" Day	93
organizational spirit	Mosaic Mascots	69
other people, learning about	Quote Quests	72
patience	Mosaic Mascots	69
	Warm Hands, Warm Hearts	143
	Banking on Goal Setting	158
	Bead Bowl	169
	Gardening	206
perseverance	Legally Blonde	38
	Banking on Goal Setting	158
personality, identifying aspects of	It's a Dog's Life	22
positive aspects of life, focusing on	Gratitude Journals	26
	The Blind Side	36
	A Raisin in the Sun	43
	Alexander and the Terrible, Horrible, No Good, Very Bad Day	49
	City of Hope	67
	Knocking Down Negativity	71
	Crush the Can'ts, Raise Your Cans	73
	Positive/Negative Word Walls	80
	"I Have a Dream" Day	93
	Rhythm and Blues	104
	April Showers Bring May Flowers	109
	Thankful Turkey	140
	Polar Express	145
	Sticks and Stones	164
	Mirror, Mirror	165
	Dream Catchers	167
	Concrete Block/Stepping Stone	210
	Positive Planter	221
	Positive Words Rock Garden	223
	Positive Words Beading	224
pride vs. humility	If	47

	The Wizard of Oz	*40*
	Soul Shine Sunshine	*81*
problems, dealing with	Bead Meaning Bracelets	*82*
	The Butterfly Story	*162*
	Umbrella of Peace	*236*
rapport between counselor and child	Initially Yours	*20*
	It's a Dog's Life	*22*
reading	Stories and Snacks	*33*
rejection, dealing with	*A Raisin in the Sun*	*43*
	Stories and Snacks	*33*
	Take a (Spring) Break and Relax	*107*
	Sand Art	*128*
	Positive Parachute	*160*
relaxation	Gardening	*206*
	Relaxation Music	*229*
	Sand Art	*230*
	Aromatherapy	*231*
	Group Sand Castles	*232*
	Mean Girls	*45*
	Positive Word Wall	*192*
respect	Create a Group Totem Pole	*198*
	Kite Decorating and Flying	*205*
	Bead Buddies	*225*
	Potato Sack Race	*227*
	Step by Step	*113*
responsibility	The Butterfly Story	*162*
	Gardening	*206*
rewarding positive behavior	Painted Pumpkins	*138*
safe place, creating	Covered with Love Journals	*31*
safety	Safety Spiders	*136*
school, encouraging a positive attitude towards	Back to School Survival Kit	*129*
	Tailgate Party	*132*
school, promoting unity towards	School Pride Guide	*131*
self, learning about	Quote Quests	*72*
self-acceptance	*Legally Blonde*	*38*
	Mirror, Mirror	*165*
self-awareness	*Legally Blonde*	*38*
	The Wizard of Oz	*40*
	Dream/Goal Boards	*75*
self-belief	*Polar Express*	*145*
	Dream Catchers	*167*
	Action Steps Windsocks	*168*
self-care strategies	Mirror, Mirror	*165*
self-confidence	*The Blind Side*	*36*
	The Wizard of Oz	*40*

self-esteem and self-expression	Initially Yours	20
	Gratitude Journals	26
	Journal Jars	29
	Purplicious	54
	Knocking Down Negativity	71
	Crush the Can'ts, Raise Your Cans	73
	Color Coding	74
	Soul Shine Sunshine	81
	Social Butterflies	87
	"I Have a Dream" Day	93
	Recipe for Success/"When Dreams Come True" Day	95
	Stuffed with Love	100
	Peaceful Earth	110
	Growing a Garden of Mental Health	111
	Step by Step	113
	Bead Buddies	115
	Sand Art	128
	Back to School Survival Kit	129
	Thankful Turkey	140
	Sticks and Stones	164
	Mirror, Mirror	165
	Bead Bowl	169
	Create a Group Totem Pole	198
	Carousel Ride and Face Painting	202
	Kite Decorating and Flying	205
	Concrete Block/Stepping Stone	210
	Bead Buddies	225
	Stuffed with Love	226
	Potato Sack Race	227
	Taste Test	228
	Sand Art	230
	Aromatherapy	231
self-expression	Picture Prompts	18
	Quote Quests	72
	Creative Cookbook	84
	Chinese Dragons	90
	April Showers Bring May Flowers	109
	Painted Pumpkins	138
	Carousel Ride and Face Painting	202
	Kite Decorating and Flying	205
self-knowledge	Anger-Control Totem Poles	116
self-soothing	Take a (Spring) Break and Relax	107
	Positive Planter	221
	Relaxation Music	229
	Sand Art	230
self-talk, positive vs. negative	Positive/Negative Word Walls	80
	Positive Word Wall	192
sincerity	*If*	47

	Journal Jars	*29*
	Journal Jams	*30*
	"Beanie Baby" Beginnings	*34*
	Mean Girls	*45*
	The True Story of the Three Little Pigs	*52*
	Enemy Pie	*57*
	Rainbow Fish	*60*
	Zoo Crew/Jungle People	*83*
	Creative Cookbook	*84*
	Social Butterflies	*87*
	"I Have a Dream" Day	*93*
	Recipe for Success/"When Dreams Come True" Day	*95*
	Stuffed with Love	*100*
	Rhythm and Blues	*104*
	Black History Program	*105*
	Pot of Gold Scavenger Hunt	*106*
	Peaceful Earth	*110*
	Growing a Garden of Mental Health	*111*
	Step by Step	*113*
	Bead Buddies	*115*
	Group Sand Castles	*127*
	Sand Art	*128*
social skills	School Pride Guide	*131*
	Tailgate Party	*132*
	Safety Spiders	*136*
	Painted Pumpkins	*138*
	Giving Back Baskets	*142*
	Sticks and Stones	*164*
	Excellent Egg Relay Race	*166*
	Bead Bowl	*169*
	Create a Group Totem Pole	*198*
	Carousel Ride and Face Painting	*202*
	Silent and Verbal Water Balloon Toss	*203*
	Kite Decorating and Flying	*205*
	"Great," "Could-Be-Better," and "Unacceptable" Behavior Bean Bag Toss	*207*
	Concrete Block/Stepping Stone	*210*
	Bead Buddies	*225*
	Stuffed with Love	*226*
	Potato Sack Race	*227*
	Taste Test	*228*
	Sand Art	*230*
	Group Sand Castles	*232*
	Peacing it Together	*234*
	Umbrella of Peace	*236*
	Peace Sign Design	*238*
sportsmanship	Potato Sack Race	*227*

stressful times, coping with	April Showers Bring May Flowers	109
	Positive Word Wall	192
supporting others	Poster Goal Commitment	161
table manners	Taste Test	228
teamwork	*Enemy Pie*	57
	City of Hope	67
	Knocking Down Negativity	71
	Rhythm and Blues	104
	Black History Program	105
	Pot of Gold Scavenger Hunt	106
	Group Cheers/Chants	157
	Positive Parachute	160
	Mirror, Mirror	165
	Excellent Egg Relay Race	166
upsetting situations, ways of responding to	Scaring Away Bad Behavior	139
viewpoints, understanding two	*The True Story of the Three Little Pigs*	52
visual reminder of therapeutic topics	Bead Meaning Bracelets	82
yourself, importance of being	*Mean Girls*	45
	Removing the Mask	78